# SUNDAY

## IS

# FAMILY DINNERS

from Roast Chicken and Mashed Potatoes to Apple Pie and More

◆ ◆ ◆

TIME®
LIFE
BOOKS

TIME-LIFE BOOKS, ALEXANDRIA, VIRGINIA

TIME-LIFE BOOKS IS A DIVISION OF TIME LIFE INC.

TIME-LIFE CUSTOM PUBLISHING

| | |
|---|---|
| Vice President and Publisher | Terry Newell |
| Project Manager | Jennifer Pearce |
| Director of Sales | Neil Levin |
| Director of New Product Development | Regina Hall |
| Managing Editor | Donia Ann Steele |
| Production Manager | Carolyn Mills Bounds |
| Quality Assurance Manager | Miriam P. Newton |

Produced by Rebus, Inc.
New York, New York

Illustrations
William Neeper

Library of Congress Cataloging-in-Publication Data
Sunday is family dinners : from roast chicken and mashed potatoes to apple pie and more/
from the editors of Time-Life Books.
p. cm. -- (The everyday cookbooks)
Includes index.
ISBN 0-7835-4789-7
ISBN 0-7835-4826-5
1. Dinners and dining.   2. Quick and easy cookery.   I. Time-Life
Books.   II. Series.
TX737.S89    1996
641.5'55--dc20
95-51347
CIP

Books produced by Time-Life Custom Publishing are available
at special bulk discount for promotional and premium use.
Custom adaptations can also be created to meet
your specific marketing goals.
Call 1-800-323-5255.

# INTRODUCTION

"Sunday Dinner" calls to mind warm family gatherings and leisurely meals, complete with the rich aromas and hearty flavors that only time at the stove can produce. In our faster-paced world, those occasions are nostalgic memories. But with the help of this cookbook, you can bring back many a savory, old-fashioned dinner to the table. Imagine main courses such as Chicken Pot Pie, Yankee Pot Roast, or Roast Pork Loin with Sage. Picture dishes like Garlic Mashed Potatoes, Cheddar Drop Biscuits, and Marinated Tomato and Red Onion Salad on the side. You'll find more than 100 classic recipes, updated for today's tastes.

To make your day easier, this cookbook includes the following features:

•The recipes are organized by menu categories—from "Main Courses" through "Side Dishes and Salads" to "Desserts"—for easy planning. Recipes call for readily-available supermarket ingredients and pantry staples.

•A special "Company's Coming" section offers more formal meals—like London Broil with Red Wine Marinade—perfect for fancier weekend cooking.

•"Menu Suggestions" gives festive menu ideas when you want to invite a few guests to join your family dinner. To accommodate extra visitors, just multiply the yields of the recipes, using each menu as a handy guide.

•"Extra-Quick" recipes, with preparation times of 45 minutes or less, are marked with this symbol: 🕐 (A full listing of these recipes is included in the index under the name Extra-Quick.)

•Recipes that get fewer than 30 percent of their calories from fat are labeled "Low-Fat" and are marked with this symbol: ♡ (A full listing of these recipes is included in the index under the name Low-Fat.)

Sitting down to a home-cooked meal with family and friends is a welcome relief from our all-too-busy lives. *Sunday Is Family Dinners* reaffirms the joy of cooking for loved ones—and the pleasure of sharing good food.

—*Mara Reid Rogers,*
*author of numerous cookbooks and*
*spokesperson for The Everyday Cookbooks*

# Contents

# DESSERTS

# COMPANY'S COMING

# MENU SUGGESTIONS

# INDEX

# MAIN COURSES

# ROAST CHICKEN WITH STUFFING

SERVES 4

♡ LOW-FAT

9 SLICES WHITE BREAD, CUT INTO
  ½-INCH CUBES
2 TEASPOONS VEGETABLE OIL
1 LARGE ONION, DICED
2 CELERY RIBS, HALVED LENGTHWISE
  AND CUT INTO THIN SLICES
3 GARLIC CLOVES, MINCED

1½ CUPS CHICKEN BROTH, PREFERABLY
  REDUCED-SODIUM
1 TEASPOON TARRAGON
1 TEASPOON ROSEMARY
½ TEASPOON SALT
ONE 3½-POUND WHOLE CHICKEN
2 TABLESPOONS FRESH LEMON JUICE

**1.** Preheat the oven to 375°. Spread the bread cubes on a baking sheet and bake for 7 minutes, stirring occasionally, or until crisp. Transfer to a large bowl.

**2.** In a large nonstick skillet, warm the oil over medium heat. Add the onion, celery, and garlic and cook, stirring frequently, until the vegetables are tender, about 7 minutes. Add to the bread along with 1¼ cups of the broth, ½ teaspoon of the tarragon, ½ teaspoon of the rosemary, and the salt. Toss well.

**3.** With your fingers, carefully loosen the skin from the chicken breast, leaving the skin intact. Rub the lemon juice under the skin, rubbing it into the meat, then rub in the remaining ½ teaspoon tarragon and remaining ½ teaspoon rosemary. Loosely spoon about ⅓ of the stuffing into the chicken cavity. Truss the chicken by tying the legs together with string. Spoon the remaining stuffing into an 8- x 8-inch baking dish, cover with foil, and set aside.

**4.** Place the chicken on a rack in a small roasting pan and roast for 20 minutes. Brush with some of the remaining ¼ cup broth and continue to roast for 1¼ hours, brushing every 15 minutes with broth, or until the chicken is cooked through. During the last 30 minutes of roasting, place the stuffing in the oven with the chicken.

**5.** Spoon the stuffing into a serving bowl and place the chicken on a platter. Remove the skin from the chicken before eating.

# Pennsylvania Dutch Chicken

SERVES 4

ONE 3-POUND CHICKEN, CUT INTO
  8 SERVING PIECES
½ CUP APPLE CIDER VINEGAR
PINCH OF CAYENNE PEPPER
½ TEASPOON GROUND GINGER
¼ TEASPOON GROUND CLOVES
½ CUP PLUS 2 TABLESPOONS
  VEGETABLE OIL

1 LARGE ONION, SLICED
1 LEMON, SLICED
1 CUP FLOUR
½ TEASPOON SALT
¼ TEASPOON BLACK PEPPER
PARSLEY SPRIGS, FOR GARNISH

**1.** Arrange the chicken in a single layer in a large shallow baking dish. Pour the vinegar over the chicken and turn to coat the pieces. Sprinkle the cayenne pepper, ginger, and cloves over the chicken, drizzle on the 2 tablespoons of oil, and cover with the onion and lemon slices. Cover the dish and let the chicken marinate for 30 minutes. Turn the chicken in the marinade often.

**2.** In a large skillet, heat the remaining oil over high heat. Remove the chicken from the marinade. Put the flour on a flat plate. Dredge the chicken in the flour and shake off any excess. The chicken should be just lightly coated.

**3.** Cook the chicken pieces in the hot oil, turning with tongs to brown evenly. When the chicken is a deep crusty brown, reduce the heat to medium and cover. Move the white pieces on top of the dark meat, which takes longer to cook. After about 10 minutes, check the white meat for doneness with the tip of a knife. (The juice should run clear.) Transfer the breasts to a heatproof platter lined with paper towels and keep warm in a preheated 200° oven.

**4.** Cover the skillet and continue to cook the dark meat for about 20 minutes, or until tender and the juices run clear.

**5.** Drain the chicken on paper towels and arrange the pieces on a serving platter. Season the chicken with the salt and pepper, and garnish with parsley sprigs.

# SOUTHERN FRIED CHICKEN

SERVES 4

🕐 EXTRA-QUICK

½ CUP FLOUR

1½ TEASPOONS SALT

½ TEASPOON BLACK PEPPER

⅓ CUP BUTTERMILK

ONE 2½-POUND CHICKEN, CUT INTO
    PIECES

⅓ CUP LARD

5 TABLESPOONS BUTTER

LEMON WEDGES AND WATERCRESS, FOR
    GARNISH

**1.** Put the flour, salt, and pepper in a paper bag and shake to combine.

**2.** Pour the buttermilk into a medium bowl and dip each piece of chicken in it to coat. Place 1 or 2 chicken pieces in the bag and shake to coat with flour. Place the coated pieces of chicken on a plate. Repeat until all of the chicken pieces are coated.

**3.** In a large skillet, warm the lard with the butter over high heat until a small cube of bread dropped in the skillet rises to the surface surrounded by bubbles.

**4.** Add the thighs and legs, fleshy side down, to the skillet. Brown about 3 minutes. When golden, turn the chicken pieces with tongs.

Add the chicken breasts to the pan. After about 3 minutes, turn all the chicken pieces. Add the wings to the pan.

**5.** Continue cooking and turning pieces so that they brown evenly. If the chicken is browning too fast, reduce the heat. All of the chicken should be done in 20 to 30 minutes from the time the thighs and legs were placed in the pan. When done, the chicken should be medium brown and the crust very crisp.

**6.** With tongs, transfer the chicken pieces to a paper-towel-lined platter to drain.

**7.** Serve the chicken on a platter garnished with the lemon wedges and watercress.

**SUBSTITUTION:** *Some Southern cooks would insist that you can't make good fried chicken without lard—and it does, indeed, add a distinctive flavor. But substitute vegetable shortening, if you prefer.*

# CHICKEN POT PIE

SERVES 6 TO 8

1¾ CUPS FLOUR

¼ CUP GRATED PARMESAN CHEESE

2 TABLESPOONS MINCED PARSLEY

½ TEASPOON SALT

8 TABLESPOONS BUTTER

2 CUPS CHICKEN BROTH

¼ POUND SMALL WHITE ONIONS,
    QUARTERED

2 CUPS PEELED, DICED SWEET POTATO

1 TEASPOON SAGE

¼ TEASPOON BLACK PEPPER

2 MEDIUM CARROTS, CUT INTO
    ¼-INCH ROUNDS

2 CUPS BROCCOLI FLORETS

½ CUP DICED CELERY

3 CUPS COOKED CHICKEN, CUT INTO
    BITE-SIZE PIECES

1 EGG, BEATEN

**1.** In a large bowl, combine 1½ cups of the flour, the Parmesan, parsley, and salt. Cut the butter in until the mixture resembles coarse meal. Work 3 tablespoons of ice water into the dough, adding up to 1 more tablespoon, until the dough forms a ball. Divide the dough in half, press each portion into a disc shape, wrap in plastic wrap, and refrigerate for at least 30 minutes.

**2.** Meanwhile, in a large saucepan, bring the chicken broth to a boil over medium-high heat. Add the onions, sweet potato, sage, and pepper, and cook for 5 minutes. Add the carrots, broccoli, and celery, and cook until the vegetables are just tender, about 5 minutes.

**3.** In a small bowl, blend the remaining flour with ¼ cup of cold water. Increase the heat under the saucepan to high, add the flour-

water mixture to the saucepan, and cook, stirring constantly, until the sauce has thickened slightly. Remove the pan from the heat and stir in the chicken.

**4.** Preheat the oven to 425°. Roll one half of the dough into a 12-inch circle and fit it into a 9-inch pie pan, letting the extra dough hang over the edges. Spoon the filling into the pastry shell. Roll the other half of the dough into a 9-inch circle and place it on top of the filling. Fold the overhang in over the top crust, crimping to seal. Cut steam vents in the top crust and brush with the beaten egg.

**5.** Bake the pie for 15 minutes. Lower the oven temperature to 325° and bake for 10 to 15 minutes, or until the crust is golden. Serve the pot pie hot.

# FRICASSEE OF CHICKEN WITH PAPRIKA

SERVES 4

4 TABLESPOONS UNSALTED BUTTER
2½ TO 3 POUNDS CHICKEN PARTS
4 MEDIUM LEEKS, COARSELY CHOPPED
2 TABLESPOONS PAPRIKA
3 CUPS CHICKEN BROTH
1 CUP DRY WHITE WINE

¼ TEASPOON SALT
⅛ TEASPOON BLACK PEPPER
8 OUNCES EGG NOODLES
3 EGG YOLKS
⅔ CUP HEAVY CREAM

**1.** Bring a large pot of water to a boil over high heat.

**2.** In a large skillet, warm the butter over medium heat until melted. Add the chicken, skin-side down, reduce the heat to medium-low, and cook, turning often, about 10 minutes. The chicken should not brown.

**3.** With tongs, transfer the chicken to a large plate. Add the leeks and paprika to the skillet, stir, and cook, covered, for 10 minutes. Stir in the broth, wine, salt, and pepper. Return the chicken to the skillet and bring the liquid to a boil. Reduce the heat to medium-low, and simmer, partially covered, for 30 minutes, basting often and turning the chicken once.

**4.** Meanwhile, add the noodles to the boiling water and cook about 9 minutes, or according to packages directions.

**5.** In a medium bowl, whisk together the egg yolks and cream. Whisking constantly, add 2 cups of hot chicken cooking liquid to the yolk mixture in a slow, steady stream.

**6.** Pour the egg mixture into the skillet, reduce the heat to low, and cook, stirring gently and turning the chicken occasionally, about 5 minutes, or until the sauce thickens. Do not let the sauce boil or it will curdle.

**7.** Serve the fricassee over the noodles.

**KITCHEN NOTE:** *Resist the temptation to skip a step by adding the egg yolks and cream directly to the pan: The yolks will curdle (think of scrambled eggs) if subjected to such high heat. That's why you must first "temper" the eggs by whisking in the hot pan juices.*

# CRISPY BEER-BATTER FRIED CHICKEN

SERVES 4

🕐 EXTRA-QUICK

1 GARLIC CLOVE, MINCED

⅔ CUP FLOUR

¼ TEASPOON BAKING POWDER

½ TEASPOON SALT

¼ TEASPOON PAPRIKA

⅓ CUP BEER

1 EGG, AT ROOM TEMPERATURE

4 CUPS VEGETABLE OIL

ONE 3½-POUND FRYING CHICKEN, CUT
  INTO PIECES OR 3½ POUNDS
  CHICKEN PARTS

4 LEMON SLICES, FOR GARNISH

4 PARSLEY SPRIGS, FOR GARNISH

**1.** In a large bowl, combine the garlic, flour, baking powder, salt, and paprika and stir to blend.

**2.** In a small bowl, combine the beer, egg, and 1 tablespoon of the oil and beat lightly with a fork until well blended. Add the beer mixture to the dry ingredients and stir until blended.

**3.** Heat the remaining oil in a very large, deep skillet over medium-high heat until a small cube of bread dropped in the oil rises to the surface surrounded by bubbles.

**4.** Dip the chicken in the beer batter, several pieces at a time, and turn to coat evenly. With tongs, transfer the chicken pieces to the skillet, allowing any excess batter to drip off before carefully lowering the chicken into the hot oil. Fry 2 minutes on each side. Continue to fry the chicken 15 minutes more on each side.

**5.** With tongs, transfer the chicken pieces to a paper-towel-lined platter to drain.

**6.** Divide the chicken pieces among 4 dinner plates and garnish each with a lemon slice and a parsley sprig.

# HONEY-ROASTED TURKEY WITH SWEET POTATO STUFFING

SERVES 12

4 NAVEL ORANGES, THE ZEST OF 2 CUT INTO FINE STRIPS

6 MEDIUM SWEET POTATOES, PEELED AND CUT INTO ½-INCH CUBES

6 TABLESPOONS UNSALTED BUTTER

3 LARGE ONIONS, CHOPPED

¼ CUP FRESH LEMON JUICE

½ CUP CHICKEN BROTH

½ TEASPOON SALT

¼ TEASPOON BLACK PEPPER

½ TEASPOON GROUND CLOVES

¾ TEASPOON DRY MUSTARD

6 SLICES WHOLE-WHEAT BREAD, CUT INTO CUBES AND LIGHTLY TOASTED

2 TABLESPOONS BRANDY

ONE 12-POUND TURKEY

¼ CUP HONEY

**1.** Blanch the orange zest in boiling water for 1 minute. Drain and set aside. Peel the oranges and divide them into sections. Cut each section in half and reserve.

**2.** In a large saucepan, blanch the sweet potatoes in boiling water for 3 minutes. Drain and set aside.

**3.** In a large casserole, melt the butter over medium-low heat Add the onion and cook until translucent, about 10 minutes. Add the orange zest, oranges, sweet potatoes, lemon juice, broth, salt, and pepper. Cook until the sweet potato cubes are tender, 7 to 10 minutes. Remove from the heat and add the cloves, mustard, bread cubes, and brandy. Mix thoroughly.

**4.** Preheat the oven to 350°. Loosely fill both cavities of the turkey with the stuffing. Tie the drumsticks together with string and tuck the wing tips under the bird. Put the turkey on a rack in a shallow roasting pan. Add 1 cup of water to the pan.

**5.** Make a tent of foil over the turkey and roast for 2½ hours. Take the turkey from the oven and remove the foil. Brush the turkey all over with the honey. Reduce the oven temperature to 325°, then roast uncovered for 1 hour. The turkey is done when a meat thermometer inserted in the thickest part of the thigh reads 180°.

**6.** Let the turkey stand for at least 20 minutes before carving it.

# ROAST BREAST OF TURKEY WITH FRUIT STUFFING

SERVES 8

♡ LOW-FAT

2 TABLESPOONS UNSALTED BUTTER

⅓ CUP FINELY CHOPPED ONION

1 LARGE TART GREEN APPLE, PEELED AND DICED

1 TEASPOON SUGAR

1 TEASPOON CHOPPED FRESH SAGE, OR ¼ TEASPOON DRIED

¼ TEASPOON GROUND CLOVES

⅓ CUP SEEDLESS RAISINS

4 OUNCES DRIED APRICOTS, CUT INTO SMALL PIECES

3 TABLESPOONS CHICKEN BROTH

¼ CUP APPLE CIDER

ONE 2-POUND BONELESS TURKEY BREAST HALF, WITH SKIN

⅛ TEASPOON SALT

1 TABLESPOON SAFFLOWER OIL

CHOPPED PARSLEY, FOR GARNISH

**I.** In a large saucepan, warm the butter over medium heat until melted. Sauté the onion until it is translucent, about 10 minutes. Add the apple and sugar and continue cooking, stirring occasionally, until the apple is tender, about 5 minutes. Stir in the sage, cloves, raisins, apricots, broth, and apple cider. Reduce the heat and cover the pan. Cook until all of the liquid is absorbed, stirring once. Transfer to a bowl and allow to cool.

**2.** Preheat the oven to 350°. Put the turkey, skin-side down, on a work surface. With a sharp knife, cut a flap in the breast by slicing from the long, thin side toward the thicker side, being careful not to cut all the way through. Open the flap and place the turkey between two pieces of plastic wrap. Pound lightly to flatten to an even thickness of about ½ inch. Sprinkle the turkey with the salt and mound the fruit stuffing in the center. Wrap the flap around the stuffing and roll the breast snugly to form a cylinder with the skin on the outside. Tuck in the ends and tie securely with string.

**3.** In a roasting pan, warm the oil over medium heat. Place the turkey in the pan, skin-side down, and brown for 3 to 4 minutes. Turn the turkey over and roast in the oven for 25 minutes, or until the juices run clear when the meat is pierced with the tip of a knife.

**4.** Cut the turkey into ¾-inch slices. Arrange on a platter and garnish with the parsley.

# ROAST PORK LOIN WITH SAGE

SERVES 6

2 TABLESPOONS OLIVE OIL

6 GARLIC CLOVES

¼ CUP CHOPPED FRESH CORIANDER, OR
   1 TABLESPOON DRIED

1 TABLESPOON SAGE

1 TEASPOON SALT

1 TEASPOON BLACK PEPPER

ONE 4-POUND CENTER-CUT BONELESS
   PORK LOIN

**1.** Preheat the oven to 450°.

**2.** In a small bowl, combine 1 tablespoon of the oil, the garlic, coriander, sage, salt, and pepper, and mash the mixture to a paste.

**3.** Rub the remaining 1 tablespoon of oil all over the pork loin, then rub the garlic mixture over the surface of the meat. Place the pork loin in a shallow roasting pan and pour in ½ cup of water. Place the pork loin in the oven and roast it for 20 to 25 minutes, basting several times.

**4.** Reduce the oven temperature to 325° and roast the pork for 1 to 1¼ hours, or until a meat thermometer registers 165 to 170°.

**5.** Let the pork stand at room temperature for 5 minutes before carving.

**KITCHEN NOTE:** *If you're lucky enough to end up with leftovers, you're all set for mouth-watering second-day sandwiches: Line slices of lightly toasted sourdough bread with Romaine, then top them with thin slices of the pork and roasted peppers.*

# Ham Loaf

### SERVES 4

1 CUP FRESH BREAD CRUMBS

½ CUP HEAVY CREAM

1 POUND GROUND SMOKED HAM,
   PREFERABLY RAW

½ POUND GROUND VEAL SHOULDER

¼ POUND GROUND PORK SHOULDER

2 EGGS

1 ONION, FINELY CHOPPED

1 GARLIC CLOVE, MASHED TO A PURÉE

2 TABLESPOONS CHOPPED PARSLEY

2 TABLESPOONS MINCED CHIVES OR
   SCALLION GREENS

½ TEASPOON SAVORY

½ TEASPOON THYME

¼ TEASPOON ALLSPICE

¼ TEASPOON GROUND CLOVES

¼ TEASPOON SALT

¼ TEASPOON BLACK PEPPER

**1.** Preheat the oven to 350°.

**2.** In a small bowl, soak the bread crumbs in the cream.

**3.** In a large bowl, combine the ham, veal, pork, eggs, onion, garlic, parsley, chives, savory, thyme, allspice, cloves, salt, and pepper. Add the bread crumbs and cream, and stir to combine.

**4.** Turn the mixture into a greased loaf pan. Bake for 50 minutes to 1 hour, or until the juices run clear and the top is crusty.

**5.** Let the meat rest for 10 minutes, then unmold onto a serving platter and slice.

# PORK CHOPS WITH YAM AND SAUSAGE STUFFING

SERVES 4

1 MEDIUM YAM OR SWEET POTATO,
    PEELED AND CUT INTO CUBES
3 TABLESPOONS UNSALTED BUTTER
2 TABLESPOONS DICED ONION
¼ POUND SPICY PORK SAUSAGE
½ TEASPOON SALT
¼ TEASPOON BLACK PEPPER
1 TABLESPOON MINCED PARSLEY

1 TABLESPOON GOLDEN RAISINS
4 CENTER-CUT LOIN PORK CHOPS
    (1 INCH THICK, WITH POCKETS CUT
    FOR STUFFING)
3 TABLESPOONS VEGETABLE OIL
3 TABLESPOONS MADEIRA
½ CUP BEEF BROTH
1 TEASPOON DIJON MUSTARD

**1.** In a medium saucepan, blanch the sweet potatoes in boiling water for 3 minutes, or until barely tender. Transfer the potatoes to a large mixing bowl and mash.

**2.** In a large ovenproof skillet, warm 1 tablespoon of the butter until melted. Add the onion, crumble in the sausage, and sauté for 8 to 10 minutes over medium heat, stirring constantly, until the onion is translucent and the sausage is cooked through and lightly browned.

**3.** Transfer the onion and sausage to the mixing bowl. Add the salt, pepper, parsley, and raisins; toss to combine.

**4.** Preheat the oven to 325°.

**5.** Stuff the pork chops with the potato mixture. Close the edges with crisscrossed toothpicks. Wipe out the skillet.

**6.** Heat the oil in the skillet. Brown the pork chops on each side for 4 minutes. Pour 1 tablespoon of the Madeira over the pork chops. Cover the skillet and place in the oven to bake for 25 to 30 minutes, turning and basting the chops once or twice. Arrange the pork chops on a platter and cover loosely with foil.

**7.** Return the skillet to the top of the stove, add the broth, the remaining 2 tablespoons Madeira, and the mustard, and boil rapidly over high heat, for 2 to 3 minutes, or until the sauce has reduced to about ½ cup. Spoon the sauce over the pork chops and serve.

# SOUTHERN FRIED PORK CHOPS

SERVES 4

⏱ EXTRA-QUICK

½ CUP FLOUR

½ TEASPOON SALT

¼ TEASPOON BLACK PEPPER

1 TEASPOON PAPRIKA

4 CENTER-CUT PORK CHOPS, EACH
ABOUT ¾ INCH THICK

¼ CUP VEGETABLE OIL

**1.** Combine the flour, salt, pepper, and paprika on a flat plate. Dredge the pork chops in the flour mixture, shaking off the excess.

**2.** In a large skillet, warm the oil over medium-high heat. Brown the pork chops in the oil for about 8 to 10 minutes on each side. Drain the pork chops on paper towels. Transfer the chops to a large serving platter. Cover loosely with foil until ready to serve.

**KITCHEN NOTE:** *For a thin, even coating on these pork chops (or any flour-dredged food), have the meat at room temperature, and pat the chops dry before dredging them in the flour mixture. For a change, you can add a pinch of dried herbs to the flour. Thyme, savory, or rosemary would be good with pork.*

# Cider-Glazed Fresh Ham

SERVES 6

ONE 6- TO 8-POUND FRESH HAM
1 TEASPOON SALT
½ TEASPOON BLACK PEPPER
24 WHOLE CLOVES

2 CUPS APPLE CIDER
1 CUP DARK BEER
3 TABLESPOONS BROWN SUGAR

**1.** Preheat the oven to 450°.

**2.** Trim the outer skin and fat from the ham, leaving ¼ inch of fat around the bone area. Rub the ham with the salt and pepper, and stud it with the garlic cloves.

**3.** Place the ham on a rack in a roasting pan, put it in the oven, and reduce the temperature to 325°. Bake the ham for 15 minutes.

**4.** Meanwhile, in a small bowl, stir together the cider, ¾ cup of the beer, and the sugar. After the ham has baked for 15 minutes, pour the cider glaze over it. Continue baking the ham, basting it with the pan juices every half hour, for 4 to 4½ hours, or until a meat thermometer inserted into the ham (not near the bone) registers 170°.

**5.** Transfer the ham to a platter and let it stand for 15 minutes before carving.

**6.** Meanwhile, to make the gravy, skim off as much fat as possible from the juices in the roasting pan. Add the remaining ¼ cup of beer and place the pan over medium heat, stirring to scrape up any browned bits clinging to the pan. Cook over low heat until hot, about 1 minute.

**7.** Carve the ham and serve it with the gravy.

**VARIATION:** *You can have a built-in side dish for this juicy roast by cooking some sweet potatoes right alongside it. Pare the potatoes and cut them into large chunks, then parboil them for about 10 minutes. Place the potatoes around the ham in the roasting pan and bake them for the last half hour of the cooking time.*

# PORK LOIN WITH POTATOES AND PEPPERS

SERVES 8

♡ LOW-FAT

⅓ CUP APPLE JUICE CONCENTRATE

3 TABLESPOONS DIJON MUSTARD

1 TABLESPOON CUMIN

¼ TEASPOON SALT

¼ TEASPOON BLACK PEPPER

1 SMALL BONELESS PORK LOIN (ABOUT 1¾ POUNDS)

18 GARLIC CLOVES

1 CUP CHICKEN BROTH

1 POUND SMALL RED POTATOES, HALVED

1 LARGE GREEN BELL PEPPER, CUT INTO THIN STRIPS

**1.** Preheat the oven to 425°.

**2.** In a small bowl, stir together the apple juice concentrate, mustard, cumin, salt, and pepper.

**3.** With a sharp knife, make 18 slits randomly in the pork loin. Tuck a clove of garlic into each slit.

**4.** Place the pork loin in a small roasting pan and brush the pork with half of the apple-mustard mixture. Pour ½ cup of broth into the bottom of the pan. Roast the pork loin for 30 minutes.

**5.** Reduce the oven temperature to 350°. Brush the pork with the remaining apple-mustard mixture and roast until it is cooked through, about 20 minutes.

**6.** Meanwhile, steam the potatoes in a vegetable steamer until almost done, about 15 minutes. Add the bell pepper to the steamer and continue steaming until the potatoes and pepper are tender, about 5 minutes. Place the vegetables in a serving bowl and cover loosely with foil.

**7.** Remove the pork from the roasting pan and let it rest for 5 minutes before slicing. Add the remaining ½ cup broth to the roasting pan and cook over medium-low heat, stirring to incorporate any browned bits clinging to the pan, for 1 to 2 minutes. Pour the pan juices over the vegetables and toss to coat.

**8.** Slice the pork, transfer to a platter, and serve with the vegetables on the side.

# CHICKEN FRIED STEAK WITH GRAVY

SERVES 4

4 BONELESS ROUND STEAKS (ABOUT 2 POUNDS TOTAL), HALVED
¾ CUP FLOUR
2 EGGS
2 TABLESPOONS MILK
12 UNSALTED SALTINE CRACKERS, FINELY CRUSHED

1½ TEASPOONS SALT
½ TEASPOON BLACK PEPPER
1 CUP PEANUT OIL
1 CUP LIGHT CREAM OR HALF-AND-HALF
1 TEASPOON WORCESTERSHIRE SAUCE
2 TABLESPOONS CHOPPED PARSLEY

**1.** Dredge the steaks in ¼ cup of the flour; set aside. Discard any unused flour.

**2.** In a shallow bowl, beat the eggs with the milk. In another shallow bowl, combine the remaining ½ cup flour with the cracker crumbs. Add 1 teaspoon of the salt and the pepper. Dip the steaks in the egg mixture and then in the seasoned flour-crumb mixture. Reserve the excess flour-crumb mixture. Set the steaks aside.

**3.** In a large skillet, warm the oil over medium-high heat. In batches, add the steaks and brown well, about 2 minutes per side.

Transfer the steaks to a platter and cover loosely with foil to keep warm.

**4.** Pour off all but 3 tablespoons of oil. Over medium heat, stir in 3 tablespoons of the reserved flour-crumb mixture, scraping up any browned bits clinging to the bottom and sides of the skillet. Add the cream and cook, stirring constantly, until slightly thickened, 1 to 2 minutes. Stir in the Worcestershire sauce, chopped parsley, and the remaining ½ teaspoon salt.

**5.** Serve the steaks topped with the gravy.

# YANKEE POT ROAST

SERVES 8

½ CUP FLOUR

1 TEASPOON SALT

½ TEASPOON BLACK PEPPER

4 POUNDS CHUCK ROAST

¼ CUP BACON DRIPPINGS (RENDERED
  FROM ABOUT ¼ POUND OF BACON)

1 TABLESPOON VEGETABLE OIL

2 CUPS BEEF BROTH

2 GARLIC CLOVES, CRUSHED

1 TEASPOON THYME

1 BAY LEAF

6 SMALL BOILING POTATOES, PEELED
  AND QUARTERED

2 OR 3 MEDIUM WHITE TURNIPS,
  PEELED AND QUARTERED

4 MEDIUM CARROTS, CUT INTO 2-INCH
  LENGTHS

¼ CUP CHOPPED PARSLEY

**1.** In a small bowl, combine the flour, salt, and pepper. Coat the roast with the seasoned flour, tapping off any excess. Reserve the remaining dredging flour.

**2.** In a Dutch oven or heatproof casserole, heat the bacon drippings and the oil over medium heat. Add the roast and brown slowly, turning to color all sides, about 30 minutes. Add more oil if necessary to prevent sticking.

**3.** Add the broth, garlic, thyme, bay leaf, and 2 cups of water to the Dutch oven. Reduce the heat to low, cover, and simmer for 2 hours, turning the roast occasionally.

**4.** Add the potatoes, turnips, and carrots, and simmer, covered, until the meat and vegetables are tender, about 30 minutes.

**5.** Remove the meat and vegetables from the Dutch oven; place on a platter and cover loosely with foil to keep warm. Discard the bay leaf.

**6.** Slowly whisk 1 cup of the pan juices into the reserved dredging flour. Place the Dutch oven over medium-high heat and whisk in the flour mixture. Bring the gravy to a boil and boil until thickened, 2 to 3 minutes. Stir in the parsley.

**7.** Slice the pot roast and serve with the vegetables and gravy.

# COUNTRY MEAT LOAF

SERVES 4 TO 6

1 POUND GROUND BEEF
½ POUND PORK SAUSAGE, CASINGS
    REMOVED
1 MEDIUM ONION, CHOPPED
¾ CUP ROLLED OATS
½ CUP KETCHUP
1 EGG, LIGHTLY BEATEN

1 TABLESPOON WORCESTERSHIRE
    SAUCE
1 TEASPOON SALT
¼ TEASPOON BLACK PEPPER
4 SLICES BACON (ABOUT ¼ POUND)
1 TABLESPOON CHOPPED PARSLEY, FOR
    GARNISH

1. Preheat the oven to 375°.

2. In a large bowl, combine the beef and sausage with the onion, oats, ketchup, egg, Worcestershire sauce, salt, and pepper.

3. Spread the meat loaf mixture evenly in a 4- x 8-inch loaf pan and pack down. Place the bacon slices side by side down the length of the meat loaf.

4. Bake the meat loaf for 30 minutes. Turn the bacon strips over and bake for another 30 minutes.

5. Slice the meat loaf and serve hot, sprinkled with the parsley.

**KITCHEN NOTE:** *The oats keep the meat loaf light textured and juicy while adding valuable dietary fiber. Add oats to other ground-meat dishes, such as burgers and meatballs, for the same benefits.*

# BEEF STROGANOFF WITH WILD MUSHROOMS

SERVES 4

⏱ EXTRA-QUICK

¾ POUND BEEF TENDERLOIN

½ OUNCE DRIED MUSHROOMS, PREFERABLY PORCINI, SOAKED IN ⅔ CUP WARM WATER FOR 20 MINUTES

2 TABLESPOONS OLIVE OIL

6 SHALLOTS, THINLY SLICED

¼ POUND MUSHROOMS, SLICED

½ TEASPOON DRIED GREEN PEPPERCORNS, CRUSHED

¼ TEASPOON SALT

3 TABLESPOONS SOUR CREAM

2 TABLESPOONS PLAIN LOW-FAT YOGURT

½ TEASPOON DIJON MUSTARD

2 TOMATOES, CUT INTO THIN STRIPS

1 SMALL SWEET PICKLE, CUT INTO SHORT THIN STRIPS

**1.** Cut the beef against the grain into ¼-inch-thick slices. Cut the slices into 1½-inch-long strips. Drain the soaked mushrooms, reserving the soaking water, and remove any remaining sand or grit under cold running water; then chop them coarsely. Strain the soaking water through a sieve lined with paper towels.

**2.** In a large nonstick skillet, warm 2 teaspoons of the oil over medium heat. Add the shallots and cook for 2 minutes, stirring, then add the dried mushrooms, soaking water, and sliced mushrooms. Cook, stirring frequently, until the excess liquid has evaporated, about 10 minutes. Remove the mushroom mixture from the pan.

**3.** Heat another 2 teaspoons of the oil in the pan over high heat and add half of the beef. Sauté for 3 to 4 minutes, stirring and tossing to brown the strips evenly. Add the browned strips to the mushroom mixture. Heat the remaining oil and brown the remaining beef strips in the same way. Return the first batch of beef and the mushroom mixture to the pan and stir. Add the peppercorns and salt.

**4.** In a small bowl, stir together the sour cream, yogurt, and mustard. Add the sour cream mixture, the tomato strips, and pickle strips to the pan. Fold together gently, but thoroughly, and heat without boiling. Serve the stroganoff hot.

# BRAISED BRISKET AND VEGETABLES

### SERVES 10

1 TABLESPOON SAFFLOWER OIL

3½ POUNDS BEEF BRISKET

1 CUP CHICKEN BROTH, PREFERABLY
   REDUCED-SODIUM

ONE 14-OUNCE CAN NO-SALT-ADDED
   TOMATOES

2 GARLIC CLOVES

½ TEASPOON SALT

10 BLACK PEPPERCORNS, CRUSHED

1 BAY LEAF

1 TABLESPOON CHOPPED FRESH THYME,
   OR 1 TEASPOON DRIED

1 LARGE CARROT, DICED

5 SMALL ONIONS, QUARTERED

1 POUND MUSHROOMS, SLICED

2 CUPS FROZEN PEAS

**1.** In a Dutch oven or heatproof casserole, warm the oil over medium-high heat. Add the brisket and brown it on all sides, then pour in the broth and enough water to cover the meat. Add the tomatoes, garlic, salt, peppercorns, bay leaf, and thyme, and bring the liquid to a boil. Reduce the heat to low, cover the Dutch oven, and simmer the beef until it feels very tender when pierced with a fork, 2 to 3 hours. Remove the brisket from the casserole, reserving the cooking liquid; keep the roast warm.

**2.** Add the carrots, onions, mushrooms, and peas to the cooking liquid. Simmer the vegetables until tender, about 20 minutes.

**3.** Remove and discard the bay leaf. Cut the brisket into neat slices and arrange them on a serving platter. Surround the meat with the vegetables. Spoon some of the cooking liquid over the brisket, and pour the rest of it into a gravy boat to be passed separately.

# BEEF PAPRIKA

SERVES 4

1¼ POUNDS BONELESS SIRLOIN STEAK,
    CUT INTO 4 PIECES
¼ TEASPOON SALT
⅛ TEASPOON BLACK PEPPER
2½ TABLESPOONS PAPRIKA
2 TABLESPOONS FLOUR
1 TABLESPOON SAFFLOWER OIL

1 ONION, CUT INTO 1-INCH CUBES
1 GREEN BELL PEPPER, CUT INTO
    1-INCH SQUARES
1 GARLIC CLOVE, FINELY CHOPPED
1½ CUPS BEEF BROTH
¼ POUND MUSHROOMS

1. Season the pieces of steak with the salt and pepper. Combine 2 tablespoons of the paprika and the flour on a plate. Dredge the steak in the flour mixture, coating each one evenly. Reserve the remaining flour mixture.

2. In a large nonstick skillet, warm 1 teaspoon of the oil over medium-high heat. Sear the meat in the skillet and set it aside. Wipe the skillet clean with a paper towel; heat the remaining 2 teaspoons of oil in it. Add the onion, bell pepper, and garlic, and sauté, stirring occasionally, until the onions are translucent, about 5 minutes. Add the remaining flour mixture, then whisk in the broth.

3. Add the steak and bring the broth to a simmer. Cover the pan and simmer the beef and vegetables for 1¼ hours. Stir in the mushrooms and the remaining ½ tablespoon of paprika; cook the mixture, covered, for 15 minutes.

4. Serve the beef surrounded by the vegetables and topped with the sauce.

**VARIATION:** *Add another dimension to this impressive dish by serving it over noodles. Toward the end of the cooking time for the meat, boil some broad egg noodles. Drain the noodles, toss them with butter and poppy seeds, and spread them on the platter; arrange the beef and vegetables on top and pour the sauce over all.*

# CORNED BEEF AND CABBAGE DINNER

### SERVES 6

4 POUNDS CORNED BEEF

1 BAY LEAF

8 PEPPERCORNS

1 GARLIC CLOVE

1 CELERY RIB, HALVED

5 MEDIUM CARROTS—2 CUT IN HALF AND 3 CUT INTO 2-INCH LENGTHS

5 MEDIUM BOILING POTATOES, PEELED AND QUARTERED

2 SMALL WHITE TURNIPS, PEELED AND QUARTERED

2 SMALL ONIONS, CUT INTO WEDGES

½ MEDIUM HEAD OF CABBAGE, CUT INTO 8 WEDGES

2 SMALL BEETS, PEELED AND QUARTERED

¼ CUP CHOPPED PARSLEY

**1.** Place the corned beef in a large soup pot or stockpot, with enough water to cover completely. Bring to a boil over high heat.

**2.** As soon as the water boils, pour it off and add fresh water to cover the corned beef. Add the bay leaf, peppercorns, garlic, celery, and halved carrots. Bring the water back to a boil over high heat, skimming any foam that rises to the surface. Reduce the heat to medium-low, cover, and simmer, skimming as necessary, until the meat is tender but still firm, about 2½ hours.

**3.** About 30 minutes before the meat is done, remove and discard the bay leaf, peppercorns, garlic, and vegetables. Add the 2-inch carrot pieces, potatoes, turnips, and onions. After 15 minutes, add the cabbage.

**4.** Meanwhile, in a medium saucepan, bring 3 cups of water to a boil. Add the beets, reduce the heat to medium-low, cover, and cook until tender, 25 to 30 minutes. Drain.

**5.** When the meat and vegetables are cooked, drain and cut the meat into slices. Arrange the meat on a platter and surround it with vegetables (including the beets). Sprinkle with the parsley and serve.

# OVEN-BARBECUED BEEF BACK RIBS

SERVES 4

🕐 EXTRA-QUICK

1 CUP KETCHUP

1 CUP BROWN SUGAR

2 TABLESPOONS CIDER VINEGAR

1 TEASPOON DRY MUSTARD

½ TEASPOON CUMIN

⅛ TEASPOON CELERY SEED

PINCH OF CAYENNE PEPPER

½ TEASPOON SALT

¼ TEASPOON BLACK PEPPER

8 TO 12 BEEF BACK RIBS (ABOUT 4 POUNDS TOTAL)

**1.** Preheat the oven to 350°.

**2.** In a medium bowl, combine the ketchup, sugar, vinegar, dry mustard, cumin, celery seed, and cayenne pepper.

**3.** Line a baking sheet with foil. Salt and pepper the ribs, and arrange in a single layer on the baking sheet. Bake for 30 minutes.

**4.** Stir the barbecue sauce to recombine and brush the ribs generously with it. Return the ribs to the oven for 10 minutes, or until they look shiny and crispy.

**5.** Transfer the ribs to a platter and pour any barbecue sauce remaining on the baking sheet over them.

**SWEET AFTERTHOUGHT:** *When the finger-lickin's finished, bring out a bowl of seasonal fresh fruit salad and light, crisp cookies. Try orange sections and blueberries, tossed with a few spoonfuls of marmalade—and some orange liqueur, if you like.*

# LAMB CHOPS WITH MUSHROOM SAUCE

SERVES 4

🕐 EXTRA-QUICK

4 TABLESPOONS BUTTER

5 OR 6 SHALLOTS, OR 1 SMALL ONION, FINELY CHOPPED

2 GARLIC CLOVES, MINCED

½ POUND MUSHROOMS, COARSELY CHOPPED

8 SMALL LAMB CHOPS (1 INCH THICK, ABOUT 2 POUNDS TOTAL)

1 TABLESPOON FLOUR

¼ CUP DRY WHITE WINE

1 TABLESPOON CHOPPED FRESH TARRAGON, OR ½ TEASPOON DRIED

½ TEASPOON SALT

¼ TEASPOON PEPPER

⅓ CUP HEAVY CREAM

3 TABLESPOONS FINE UNSEASONED DRY BREAD CRUMBS

**1.** Preheat the broiler. Line a broiler pan with foil.

**2.** In a large skillet, warm 2 tablespoons of the butter over medium-high heat until melted. Add the shallots and garlic and sauté until the shallots are translucent, about 3 minutes.

**3.** Add the remaining 2 tablespoons butter and the mushrooms and sauté until the mushrooms begin to wilt, about 3 minutes.

**4.** Broil the lamb chops on the broiler pan 4 inches from the heat for 8 minutes.

**5.** Meanwhile, add the flour to the mushrooms and stir to combine. Stir in the wine, tarragon, salt, and pepper. Bring to a boil over medium-high heat and cook for 2 minutes. Stir in the cream, reduce the heat to medium and simmer, uncovered, until the sauce has thickened slightly, about 2 minutes.

**6.** Turn the lamb chops over. Dividing evenly, spoon some mushroom sauce over each chop. Sprinkle the chops with the bread crumbs and broil 4 inches from the heat for 8 minutes for medium-rare, 10 minutes for medium, 12 minutes for well done.

# SIDE DISHES AND SALADS

# GARLIC MASHED POTATOES

SERVES 8

♡ LOW-FAT

4 TEASPOONS OLIVE OIL

4 CUPS THINLY SLICED SHALLOTS OR
   ONIONS

2 TEASPOONS SUGAR

1 CUP CHICKEN BROTH

1¼ TEASPOONS SALT

3½ POUNDS BAKING POTATOES, PEELED
   AND CUT INTO LARGE CHUNKS

16 GARLIC CLOVES, PEELED

¼ TEASPOON NUTMEG

2 BAY LEAVES

1 CUP EVAPORATED LOW-FAT MILK

**1.** In a large nonstick skillet, warm 2 teaspoons of the oil over medium heat. Add the shallots, sprinkle with the sugar, and cook, stirring frequently, until glazed, about 5 to 8 minutes. Add the broth and ¼ teaspoon of the salt. Cook, stirring occasionally, until the shallots are tender and caramelized, about 7 minutes. Remove the skillet from the heat and set aside.

**2.** Meanwhile, in a large pot, combine the potatoes, garlic, nutmeg, bay leaves, and enough cold water to cover. Bring to a boil, add ½ teaspoon of the salt, reduce to a simmer, and cook until the potatoes are tender, about 20 minutes. Drain well. Transfer the potatoes and garlic to a large bowl and discard the bay leaves.

**3.** With a potato masher or an electric mixer, mash the potatoes and garlic until smooth. Beat in the evaporated milk, the remaining 2 teaspoons of oil, and the remaining ½ teaspoon of salt, until the mixture is thick and creamy. Top the mashed potatoes with the shallot mixture, transfer to a medium bowl, and serve hot.

# SPICY BROCCOLI AND CORN CUSTARDS

SERVES 4

ONE 10-OUNCE PACKAGE FROZEN
CHOPPED BROCCOLI, THAWED
ONE 10-OUNCE PACKAGE FROZEN
CORN, THAWED
1 CUP COTTAGE CHEESE
3 EGGS
⅔ CUP SOUR CREAM
1 TABLESPOON CHILI POWDER

½ TEASPOON SALT
¼ TEASPOON BLACK PEPPER
PINCH OF CAYENNE PEPPER
2 TABLESPOONS CHOPPED CHIVES OR
SCALLION GREENS
3 TABLESPOONS GRATED PARMESAN
CHEESE

**1.** Preheat the oven to 325°. Lightly butter four 1-cup ramekins or custard cups, or a 1-quart soufflé dish.

**2.** Place the thawed frozen broccoli and corn on several layers of paper towels to drain; squeeze them in the towels if necessary to remove excess moisture.

**3.** In a food processor, purée the cottage cheese. Add the eggs, 1 at a time, and process until blended. Add the sour cream, chili powder, salt, black pepper, and cayenne pepper; process until blended.

**4.** In a medium bowl, stir together the broccoli, corn, cottage cheese-egg mixture, and the chives.

**5.** Dividing evenly, spoon the mixture into the prepared ramekins. Sprinkle the tops with the Parmesan.

**6.** Place the ramekins in a roasting pan and add hot water to come halfway up the sides of the ramekins. Place the roasting pan in the oven and bake for 45 minutes, or until a knife inserted in the center of the custard comes out clean. Serve warm, in the ramekins.

**KITCHEN NOTE:** *To microwave this dish, prepare as directed, but don't butter the ramekins. Place the filled ramekins in a circle on a large plate. Cook at Medium, rotating the plate once, until a knife inserted in the center of a custard comes out clean, 8 to 10 minutes.*

# SCALLOPED NEW POTATOES

SERVES 4 TO 6

2 TABLESPOONS FLOUR

1 TEASPOON SALT

½ TEASPOON PEPPER, PREFERABLY
    WHITE

2½ POUNDS SMALL NEW POTATOES,
    PEELED AND CUT INTO ⅛-INCH-
    THICK SLICES

1 CUP CHOPPED SCALLIONS

1 TEASPOON MINCED GARLIC

3 TABLESPOONS BUTTER

2 CUPS LIGHT CREAM OR HALF-AND-
    HALF

1. Preheat the oven to 350°. Butter a 2- to 2½-quart baking dish.

2. In a small bowl, combine the flour, salt, and pepper.

3. Layer half of the potatoes in the bottom of the prepared baking dish. Sprinkle half the scallions and garlic on top. Sprinkle evenly with the seasoned flour. Repeat with the remaining potatoes, scallions, and garlic. Dot with the butter.

4. In a small saucepan, heat the cream until steaming but not boiling. Pour the hot cream over the potatoes and bake, uncovered, until the potatoes are tender and top is browned, about 1 hour and 15 minutes.

KITCHEN NOTE: *Scalloped potatoes are best made with waxy (boiling) potatoes, which retain their firm texture during cooking. For a simple variation on this recipe, sprinkle some thyme, basil, or tarragon over the potatoes before baking.*

# Pennsylvania German-Style Broccoli

SERVES 6

🕐 EXTRA-QUICK

4 SLICES BACON

1 POUND BROCCOLI, CUT INTO BITE-
SIZE PIECES

4 SCALLIONS, COARSELY CHOPPED

1 MEDIUM RED BELL PEPPER, COARSELY
CHOPPED

⅓ CUP CIDER VINEGAR

4 TEASPOONS SPICY BROWN MUSTARD

¾ TEASPOON SUGAR

¾ TEASPOON SALT

½ TEASPOON BLACK PEPPER

2 TABLESPOONS VEGETABLE OIL

**1.** In a medium skillet, cook the bacon over medium heat until crisp, about 10 minutes. Drain the bacon on paper towels, crumble and set aside. Pour off all but 3 tablespoons of bacon fat from the pan; set the pan aside.

**2.** Meanwhile, steam the broccoli pieces in a vegetable steamer until they are crisp-tender, about 8 minutes.

**3.** Place the scallions, red pepper, and the cooked broccoli in a serving bowl.

**4.** Warm the bacon fat in the skillet over medium heat. Add the vinegar, mustard, sugar, salt, and pepper. Cook, stirring constantly to scrape up the pan drippings. Remove the skillet from the heat and stir in the oil. Pour the hot dressing over the vegetables and toss to combine.

**5.** Sprinkle the crumbled bacon over the broccoli and serve.

# PARMESAN POTATOES

SERVES 6

🕐 EXTRA-QUICK

12 SMALL RED POTATOES, SLICED

4 GARLIC CLOVES

½ CUP PLUS 2 TABLESPOONS GRATED
   PARMESAN CHEESE

4 TABLESPOONS BUTTER

2 TABLESPOONS MILK

½ TEASPOON SALT

¼ TEASPOON PEPPER, PREFERABLY
   WHITE

2 TABLESPOONS CHOPPED PARSLEY
   (OPTIONAL)

**1.** Bring a 3-quart saucepan of water to a boil. Add the potatoes and garlic cloves to the boiling water and cook until the potatoes are tender, about 15 minutes.

**2.** Preheat the broiler. Butter a shallow 1-quart baking dish.

**3.** Drain the potatoes and garlic well. Slip the garlic cloves out of their skins.

**4.** In a shallow bowl, coarsely mash the potatoes and garlic with a potato masher or a fork (do not use a food processor; it will make the potatoes gluey).

**5.** Add ½ cup of the Parmesan, the butter, milk, salt, and pepper to the mashed potatoes and mix thoroughly. Spread the potatoes in the prepared baking dish and sprinkle the remaining 2 tablespoons Parmesan evenly on top.

**6.** Broil the potatoes 4 inches from the heat for 6 minutes, or until the top is lightly browned.

**7.** Serve the potatoes garnished with the chopped parsley, if desired.

# GLAZED CARROT COINS

SERVES 4

🕐 EXTRA-QUICK

⅓ CUP APPLE JUICE

3 TABLESPOONS BUTTER

2 TEASPOONS BROWN SUGAR

¼ TEASPOON SALT

6 LARGE CARROTS, THINLY SLICED

1 TABLESPOON CHOPPED PARSLEY
   (OPTIONAL)

**1.** In a medium saucepan, bring the apple juice, butter, and brown sugar to a boil over medium-high heat. Stir in the salt.

**2.** Add the carrots, reduce the heat to medium, cover, and simmer, stirring occasionally, until the carrots are tender, 5 to 8 min-utes. If there is a lot of liquid in the pan, cook the carrots uncovered for the last minute or so to reduce the cooking liquid to a glaze.

**3.** Toss the carrots with the parsley, if desired, and serve.

**VARIATION:** *Treat the family to orange-glazed carrots for a change: Substitute orange juice for the apple juice, and toss the glazed carrots with chopped fresh mint instead of parsley.*

# CAULIFLOWER-CHEDDAR GRATIN

SERVES 6

⏲ EXTRA-QUICK

1 SMALL HEAD OF CAULIFLOWER, BROKEN INTO FLORETS
2 TABLESPOONS BUTTER
½ CUP FINE UNSEASONED DRY BREAD CRUMBS
½ TEASPOON OREGANO
¼ TEASPOON SALT
¼ TEASPOON PEPPER
⅓ CUP GRATED CHEDDAR CHEESE

**1.** Pour enough water into a saucepan to fill it 1 inch deep. Set a vegetable steamer in the pan and bring the water to a boil. Put the cauliflower in the steamer, cover, and steam for 10 to 12 minutes, or until tender.

**2.** Meanwhile, preheat the broiler.

**3.** Melt the butter on the stovetop or in the microwave.

**4.** In a medium bowl, combine the bread crumbs, oregano, salt, and pepper. Stir in the melted butter and grated cheese.

**5.** In a shallow baking dish, arrange the cauliflower florets in a single layer. Sprinkle the cheese-crumb mixture over the top.

**6.** Broil the cauliflower 4 inches from the heat for 2 minutes, or until golden on top.

**KITCHEN NOTE:** *You don't need a porcelain gratin dish for this recipe; a metal baking pan will do, although you may want to line it with foil for easier cleanup.*

# BRUSSELS SPROUTS WITH CARAMELIZED ONION

SERVES 4

♡ LOW-FAT

1 LARGE ONION, THINLY SLICED
1 TABLESPOON OLIVE OIL
⅛ TEASPOON SALT
PINCH OF BLACK PEPPER

1 CUP DRY WHITE WINE
1 POUND BRUSSELS SPROUTS, CUT IN HALF

**1.** In a medium saucepan, combine the onion, oil, salt, pepper, and ½ cup of water and bring to a boil, partially covered, over high heat. Reduce the heat to medium and cook, stirring occasionally, for 1 hour, or until the onion is caramelized.

**2.** Uncover the pan and add the wine to the onion, Raise the heat to high and boil rapidly for 5 to 10 minutes, or until almost all of the wine has evaporated.

**3.** About 15 minutes before the onion is done, steam the Brussels sprouts. Pour enough water into a saucepan to fill it 1 inch deep. Set a vegetable steamer in the pan and bring the water to a boil. Place the Brussels sprouts in the steamer, cover the pan tightly, and steam the sprouts for 5 minutes, or until tender.

**4.** Toss the caramelized onion with the Brussels sprouts and serve.

# WAX BEANS AND CHERRY TOMATOES

SERVES 6

⊕ EXTRA - QUICK

1 POUND WAX BEANS, TRIMMED

2 TABLESPOONS OLIVE OIL

1 SMALL ONION, THINLY SLICED

1 GARLIC CLOVE, FINELY CHOPPED

1 CUP CHERRY TOMATOES, HALVED

2 TABLESPOONS CHOPPED FRESH BASIL, PLUS SEVERAL WHOLE LEAVES, FOR GARNISH

¼ TEASPOON SALT

PINCH OF BLACK PEPPER

**1.** Pour enough water into a saucepan to fill it about an inch deep. Set a vegetable steamer in the pan and bring the water to a boil. Put the beans in the steamer, cover the pan, and steam the beans for 5 to 7 minutes, or until they are tender, but still crisp.

**2.** In a large skillet, warm the oil over medium heat. Add the onion and garlic and cook 2 to 3 minutes, or until the onions are soft. Add the beans and cook, stirring occasionally, for 2 minutes. Add the tomatoes, basil, salt, and pepper. Stir well and continue cooking for about 2 minutes, or until the tomatoes are heated through.

**3.** Transfer the vegetables to a serving dish and garnish with the whole basil leaves. Serve immediately.

**VARIATION:** *You could further brighten this already colorful dish by using half green beans and half wax beans, and a mixture of red and yellow cherry and pear tomatoes.*

# FRIED GREEN TOMATOES

SERVES 4

🕐 EXTRA-QUICK

1 CUP FLOUR

¼ TEASPOON SALT

¼ TEASPOON BLACK PEPPER

4 LARGE GREEN OR NOT-TOO-RIPE RED
    TOMATOES, CUT INTO THICK SLICES

1 TABLESPOON SUGAR

6 TABLESPOONS UNSALTED BUTTER

¾ CUP HEAVY CREAM

2 TABLESPOONS CHOPPED FRESH
    PARSLEY, FOR GARNISH (OPTIONAL)

**1.** Put the flour, salt, and pepper on a flat plate and stir to combine. Dredge the tomato slices in the flour to coat each well; shake off any excess. Sprinkle sugar on both sides of the tomato slices.

**2.** In a medium skillet, warm 2 tablespoons of the butter over medium-high heat. Brown a few tomato slices at a time for 1 to 2 minutes on each side, or until crispy. Transfer the tomato slices to a heatproof platter and keep warm in the oven. Add more butter to the pan as needed and continue to brown the tomato slices on both sides until all are done.

**3.** Add the cream to the pan and bring to a boil. Scrape the pan with a wooden spoon to loosen any brown bits on the bottom. Cook, stirring constantly, for 10 minutes, or until the cream is slightly reduced.

**4.** Remove the tomatoes from the oven and pour the sauce over them. Sprinkle with the chopped parsley, if desired.

# BAKED CORN

SERVES 4

2 CUPS FROZEN CORN KERNELS,
   THAWED
2 TEASPOONS CHOPPED FRESH DILL, OR
   1 TEASPOON DRIED
3 LARGE EGGS

1 TEASPOON SALT
1 CUP HEAVY CREAM
ADDITIONAL CHOPPED FRESH DILL, FOR
   GARNISH (OPTIONAL)

**1.** Preheat the oven to 350°.

**2.** Place the corn kernels in a lightly greased shallow baking dish and sprinkle the dill on top.

**3.** Place the eggs in a small bowl and, with a whisk, beat about 10 strokes. Add the salt and cream and beat to incorporate.

**4.** Pour the custard over the corn and dill and stir to combine.

**5.** Place the baking dish with the corn mixture in a larger dish. Pour enough boiling water into larger dish so that the water comes about halfway up the side of the smaller dish.

**6.** Place the dishes on the middle rack of the oven. Bake for 35 to 40 minutes, or until a knife inserted 1½ inches in from the edge of the baking dish comes out clean. The center will set after the pudding is removed from the oven.

**7.** Garnish the pudding with additional chopped fresh dill, if desired.

# CREAMED SPINACH

SERVES 4

⏱ EXTRA - QUICK

TWO 10-OUNCE PACKAGES FROZEN
   CHOPPED SPINACH
¾ TEASPOON SALT
3 TABLESPOONS UNSALTED BUTTER
3 SHALLOTS, OR 1 SMALL WHITE
   ONION, MINCED

2 TABLESPOONS FLOUR
1 CUP MILK
⅛ TEASPOON BLACK PEPPER
PINCH OF NUTMEG

**1.** In a medium saucepan, bring 2 cups of water to a boil. Add the frozen spinach and ½ teaspoon of the salt. Break up the spinach with a fork as soon as it begins to soften. Cover and simmer for 5 minutes; drain in a fine-meshed strainer. Wipe out the saucepan.

**2.** Melt the butter in the saucepan and stir in the shallots or onion. Cook over low heat for 2 to 3 minutes, or until transparent. Add the flour and cook, stirring, about 3 minutes. Remove the saucepan from the heat.

**3.** Meanwhile, in a small saucepan, bring the milk to a boil. Pour the boiling milk into the shallot mixture and beat well with a whisk to avoid lumping. Return the pan to low heat.

**4.** Squeeze any excess liquid out of the spinach and add to the sauce. Stir in the remaining ¼ teaspoon of salt, the pepper, and nutmeg.

**5.** Cover the spinach to keep warm until ready to serve.

**SUBSTITUTION:** *The shallot-flavored white sauce would be equally delicious with steamed fresh vegetables. Try it with finely shredded green cabbage or broccoli florets. If you want to use fresh spinach, you'll need 2 to 3 pounds to serve 4. Steam the spinach for 5 to 8 minutes, or until tender but still emerald green.*

# Corn with Peppers and Onion

S E R V E S   4

⏱ E X T R A - Q U I C K

2 TABLESPOONS OLIVE OIL

1 MEDIUM RED BELL PEPPER, COARSELY
   CHOPPED

1 MEDIUM GREEN BELL PEPPER,
   COARSELY CHOPPED

1 SMALL ONION, THINLY SLICED

ONE 10-OUNCE PACKAGE FROZEN
   CORN KERNELS, THAWED

¼ TEASPOON SALT

⅓ CUP CHOPPED PARSLEY

**1.** In a medium skillet, warm the oil over medium heat. Add the peppers and onion, and sauté, stirring occasionally, until the vegetables are tender but not browned, about 10 minutes.

**2.** Add the corn and salt to the vegetables in the skillet and stir to combine.

**3.** Transfer the vegetables to a bowl and cover with foil to keep warm until serving time. Just before serving, fold in the parsley.

**SUBSTITUTION:** *You can also make this simple side dish with canned or fresh corn. A 15-ounce can of whole kernel corn is roughly equivalent to 10 ounces of frozen corn. For fresh corn cut from the cob, you'll need to buy about 3 medium ears. Add the fresh corn to the skillet together with the peppers and onion, as it needs to cook for about 10 minutes.*

# CREAMED ONIONS

SERVES 6 TO 8

♡ LOW-FAT

32 SMALL WHITE ONIONS, PEELED
1 TEASPOON UNSALTED BUTTER
1 TEASPOON SUGAR
2¼ CUPS LOW-FAT MILK
2 TABLESPOONS FLOUR

½ TEASPOON THYME
¾ TEASPOON SALT
¼ TEASPOON BLACK PEPPER
¼ CUP FINELY CHOPPED PARSLEY

**1.** In a large pot of boiling water, blanch onions for 2 minutes; drain.

**2.** In a large nonstick skillet, warm the butter over low heat until melted. Add the onions, sprinkle with sugar and cook, shaking the pan frequently, until the onions are glazed and lightly golden, about 5 minutes.

**3.** In a medium saucepan, whisk together the milk, flour, thyme, salt, and pepper. Bring to a boil over medium heat. Reduce the heat to low and simmer for 5 minutes, or until lightly thickened.

**4.** Pour the white sauce over the onions. Stir in the parsley. Cover and cook over low heat for 25 minutes, or until the onions are tender. Transfer the creamed onions to a medium bowl and serve.

# GREEN BEANS
# IN SHALLOT BUTTER

### SERVES 4

### 🕐 EXTRA-QUICK

2 TABLESPOONS OLIVE OIL

2 TABLESPOONS BUTTER

½ CUP CHOPPED SHALLOTS

1 POUND GREEN BEANS, CUT INTO
   2-INCH PIECES

½ TEASPOON SALT

½ TEASPOON BLACK PEPPER

**1.** In a medium skillet, warm the oil with the butter over medium heat until the butter is melted. Add the shallots and sauté for 5 minutes, or until light golden.

**2.** Add the green beans, salt, and pepper, and sauté for 3 to 5 minutes, or until the beans are crisp-tender. Serve hot.

**VARIATION:** *When asparagus is in season, cook it in the same way as the green beans. Snap off and discard the tough bottoms from the spears, then cut what remains into 2-inch pieces, keeping the tips separate. Add the thicker pieces to the skillet first, then add the tips about 1 minute later—they're more tender than the stalks and will cook in less time.*

# GRITS AND SWISS CHEESE CASSEROLE

SERVES 6

2 CUPS MILK
⅓ CUP BUTTER
2 GARLIC CLOVES, MINCED
½ TEASPOON SALT
¼ TEASPOON BLACK PEPPER

1 CUP GRITS
2 CUPS GRATED SWISS CHEESE
1 CUP CHOPPED SCALLIONS
3 EGGS, LIGHTLY BEATEN

1. Preheat the oven to 350°. Butter a ½-quart baking dish.

2. In a large saucepan, bring 2 cups of water to a boil with the milk, butter, garlic, salt, and pepper. Gradually stir in the grits. Reduce the heat to medium-low and simmer, uncovered, stirring frequently until thick, about 5 minutes. Stir in the cheese and scallions and remove from the heat.

3. Place the eggs in a bowl. Stir about 1 cup of the hot grits into the eggs, then stir the warmed eggs into the remaining grits in the saucepan. Pour the grits into the prepared baking dish and spread evenly. Bake until the grits are set and golden brown on top, about 35 to 40 minutes.

4. Let the grits stand for 10 minutes before serving.

# STUFFED BAKED POTATOES

SERVES 4

4 LARGE BAKING POTATOES
2 TABLESPOONS BUTTER
4 TO 6 SLICES BACON (ABOUT
  ¼ POUND TOTAL)
½ CUP FINELY CHOPPED ONION
½ CUP FINELY CHOPPED GREEN BELL
  PEPPER

½ CUP CHOPPED TOMATO
¼ CUP SOUR CREAM
1 EGG YOLK
¼ TEASPOON BLACK PEPPER
1 CUP GRATED SWISS OR CHEDDAR
  CHEESE

**1.** Preheat the oven to 425°.

**2.** Prick the potatoes with the tines of a fork and rub the skins with butter. Bake until the potatoes are tender, about 1 hour.

**3.** Meanwhile, in a medium skillet, cook the bacon over medium heat until crisp, about 10 minutes. Reserving the fat in the skillet, drain the bacon on paper towels; crumble and set aside.

**4.** Add the onion to the skillet and sauté over medium heat for 5 minutes. Add the bell pepper and tomato and cook until the onion is softened but not browned, about 5 minutes. Set aside.

**5.** When the potatoes are done, remove them from the oven and lower the oven temperature to 375°. Cut a ¼-inch-thick horizontal slice from a long side of each potato. Scoop out the inside of the potato, leaving a ¼-inch shell.

**6.** Place the potato pulp in a bowl and mash it to a smooth purée with a fork. Beat in the sour cream, egg yolk, and black pepper. Stir in the reserved vegetable mixture and bacon.

**7.** Spoon the mashed potato mixture into the potato shells. Place the potatoes in a baking dish, sprinkle the cheese on top, and bake until the tops are golden brown, about 10 minutes.

# CREAMED YAMS WITH BROWN SUGAR

SERVES 6

3 POUNDS YAMS
⅛ CUP HEAVY CREAM

4 TABLESPOONS BUTTER, MELTED
3 TABLESPOONS BROWN SUGAR

**1.** In a large pot of simmering salted water, cook the yams until tender, about 30 to 35 minutes; drain. When they are just cool enough to handle, peel the yams and mash them until smooth.

**2.** Add the cream, butter, and sugar, and stir until well blended. Serve warm.

**KITCHEN NOTE:** *Although boiling is a quick way to cook sweet potatoes, baking brings out more of their natural sweetness. Before baking, scrub the potatoes and prick them several times with a fork. They'll take about 45 minutes to 1 hour in a 400° oven. If you're doing some baking and have room in the oven, put in the potatoes (the temperature isn't crucial—325° or 350° is fine) and they'll be done in the time it takes to bake a pie or several batches of cookies.*

# BOSTON BAKED BEANS

SERVES 4

♡ LOW-FAT

¼ POUND SALT PORK, DICED

1 MEDIUM ONION, CHOPPED

⅔ CUP MOLASSES

3 TABLESPOONS BROWN SUGAR

1 TABLESPOON DRY MUSTARD

1 TEASPOON SALT

½ TEASPOON BLACK PEPPER

¼ TEASPOON GROUND CLOVES

THREE 16-OUNCE CANS PINTO BEANS,
    RINSED AND DRAINED

1 BAY LEAF

**1.** In a small saucepan of boiling water, blanch the salt pork for 3 minutes. Drain and set aside.

**2.** Preheat the oven to 250°.

**3.** In a medium bowl, combine the onion, molasses, brown sugar, dry mustard, salt, pepper, and cloves. Stir in 2 cups of water.

**4.** Place the beans and the salt pork in a 2½-quart casserole or bean pot. Add the bay leaf. Pour the onion-molasses mixture over the beans. Cover tightly and bake for 30 minutes.

**5.** Remove the cover, stir the beans, and continue baking, uncovered, for 30 minutes. Discard the bay leaf before serving.

# WILD RICE WITH SCALLIONS AND RED PEPPER

SERVES 4

1 GARLIC CLOVE, MINCED

¾ CUP WILD RICE

2½ CUPS CHICKEN BROTH

4 TABLESPOONS UNSALTED BUTTER

¼ CUP CHOPPED SCALLIONS

¼ CUP DICED RED BELL PEPPER

⅛ TEASPOON SALT

PINCH OF BLACK PEPPER

**1.** In a small saucepan, combine the garlic, rice, and broth. Cover the pan and bring to a boil over high heat. Reduce the heat to low and simmer, stirring occasionally, about 40 minutes, or until all of the liquid is absorbed.

**2.** In a medium skillet, warm the butter over medium-high heat until melted. Add the scallions and pepper and sauté for 2 to 3 minutes, or until the scallions are soft and translucent.

**3.** Add the rice to the scallions and pepper and sauté, tossing and stirring frequently, 3 to 4 minutes.

**4.** Add the salt and pepper, toss to combine, and transfer to a serving bowl.

**KITCHEN NOTE:** *Wild rice is not really a rice, but the seed of a grass that grows in shallow lakes. Once, all wild rice was grown in the north-central states (mainly Minnesota) and Canada, and all of it was gathered, threshed, and winnowed by hand, making it very expensive. Now, some wild rice is grown in artificial paddies in places as unlikely as California, and is processed by machine. This cultivated rice is somewhat cheaper than its "wilder" counterpart.*

# CHEDDAR DROP BISCUITS

SERVES 6 TO 8

2 CUPS FLOUR

2 TEASPOONS BAKING POWDER

¼ TEASPOON BAKING SODA

½ TEASPOON SALT

½ TEASPOON THYME

4 TABLESPOONS UNSALTED BUTTER,
  CUT INTO PIECES

1 CUP BUTTERMILK

¾ CUP SHREDDED CHEDDAR CHEESE

**1.** Preheat the oven to 450°.

**2.** Combine the flour, baking powder, baking soda, salt, and thyme in a medium bowl and stir with a fork to blend. With a pastry blender or 2 knives, cut in the butter until the mixture resembles a coarse cornmeal.

**3.** With a wooden spoon, stir in the buttermilk and ½ cup of the shredded Cheddar, and beat vigorously for 30 seconds.

**4.** Drop the batter by heaping tablespoonfuls at least 2 inches apart onto an ungreased baking sheet, making 10 to 12 biscuits. Sprinkle each biscuit with the remaining Cheddar and bake 8 to 10 minutes, or until puffed and golden.

**5.** Transfer the biscuits to a wire cooling rack. Serve warm.

# SPOON BREAD

SERVES 4

4 TABLESPOONS BUTTER

2⅓ CUPS LIGHT CREAM OR HALF-AND-HALF

1 TABLESPOON SUGAR

1 TABLESPOON HONEY

½ TEASPOON SALT

1 CUP WHITE CORNMEAL

4 EGGS, SEPARATED

1 TEASPOON BAKING POWDER

PINCH OF WHITE PEPPER

**1.** Preheat the oven to 375°.

**2.** In a medium saucepan, warm the butter with the cream, sugar, honey, and salt and cook over low heat until the butter is melted. Slowly add the cornmeal, and cook, stirring constantly, until the mixture thickens. Do not boil.

**3.** Transfer the cornmeal mixture to a large bowl. Beat in the eggs yolks, one at a time, beating well after each addition. Add the baking powder and white pepper.

**4.** In a large bowl, with an electric mixer beat the egg whites until stiff. Fold the egg whites into the cornmeal mixture. Pour into a buttered casserole or soufflé dish. Bake about 35 minutes, or until puffed and golden.

**KITCHEN NOTE:** *Despite its name, spoon bread is more akin to a soufflé than to bread. Rather than being sliced and spread with butter, it's served and eaten with a spoon. Although it's puffed with egg whites, this spoon bread—unlike a soufflé—does not need to be rushed to the table: It won't collapse if it stands for a while.*

# POPOVERS

SERVES 4

2 LARGE EGGS, AT ROOM TEMPERATURE
1 SCANT CUP FLOUR

1½ TEASPOONS SALT
1 CUP LOW-FAT MILK

**1.** Preheat the oven to 450°.

**2.** Place the eggs in a medium bowl and, with a whisk, beat thoroughly. Add the flour, salt, and milk and beat with a wooden spoon until well blended. The batter should have the consistency of heavy cream.

**3.** Butter 8 medium custard cups and place them in the oven for 4 to 5 minutes.

**4.** Fill the hot custard cups with the batter to ⅔ full and place on a cookie sheet. Bake for 25 minutes, then reduce the oven temperature to 375° and bake another 20 minutes. Do not open the oven door until the popovers are ready to be brought to the table.

# SAUTÉED APPLE SLICES

SERVES 6

⏱ EXTRA-QUICK

2 TABLESPOONS BUTTER
1 RED DELICIOUS APPLE, THINLY
   SLICED
1 GOLDEN DELICIOUS APPLE, THINLY
   SLICED

1 TABLESPOON BROWN SUGAR
¼ TEASPOON NUTMEG
2 TABLESPOONS APPLE BRANDY

**1.** In a large nonstick skillet, warm the butter over medium heat until melted. Add the apple slices and cook, stirring, until the apples begin to brown, 2 to 3 minutes.

**2.** Add the sugar, nutmeg, and brandy, and cover the pan. Reduce the heat to low and cook the apples, stirring, until just tender, 1 to 2 minutes.

**3.** Serve the apples with the pan juices spooned over them.

**Substitution:** *Apple cider or apple juice can stand in for the apple brandy in this recipe. (If you are using brandy, a French Calvados or an American applejack are two possible choices.)*

# TART APPLESAUCE

SERVES 4

♡ LOW-FAT

2 LARGE TART APPLES, PEELED AND
   COARSELY CHOPPED
½ CUP UNSWEETENED APPLE CIDER OR
   JUICE

1 TABLESPOON FRESH LEMON JUICE
1 TEASPOON HONEY

**1.** In a small saucepan, combine the apples, apple cider, lemon juice, and honey and cook over medium heat for 10 to 15 minutes, or until the apples are tender.

**2.** Purée the apple mixture in a food processor or mash with a fork. To serve warm, return the mixture to the saucepan and reheat over low heat or serve at room temperature.

**VARIATION:** *For a tart and spicy sauce, sprinkle in your choice of cinnamon, nutmeg, or allspice—with a light hand, so that the spice doesn't overpower the apples. A drop or two of vanilla extract also enhances the flavor of any applesauce.*

# CAESAR SALAD

SERVES 4

🕐 EXTRA-QUICK

2 TABLESPOONS BUTTER

2 GARLIC CLOVES—1 MINCED AND 1 LEFT WHOLE

4 SLICES WHITE BREAD, CUT INTO CUBES

1 LARGE HEAD OF ROMAINE LETTUCE

2 TABLESPOONS MAYONNAISE

2 TABLESPOON FRESH LEMON JUICE

PINCH OF BLACK PEPPER

½ CUP OLIVE OIL

8 ANCHOVY FILLETS, RINSED AND PATTED DRY

1 OUNCE PARMESAN CHEESE, GRATED

**1.** In a small saucepan, warm the butter with the minced garlic over medium-high heat until the butter is melted. Add the bread cubes and sauté, stirring occasionally, about 5 minutes, or until crisp and golden. Transfer the croutons to a paper-towel-lined plate; set aside.

**2.** Place the lettuce in a large salad bowl. Break large leaves into bite-size pieces.

**3.** In a food processor, combine the remaining clove of garlic, the mayonnaise, lemon juice, and pepper and process for 10 seconds. With the machine running, slowly drizzle the olive oil down the feed tube.

**4.** Add the dressing, the anchovies, and Parmesan to the lettuce and toss to combine.

**5.** Serve the salad topped with the croutons.

# Tossed Green Salad with Sherry Vinegar Dressing

SERVES 4

🕐 EXTRA-QUICK

2 TO 3 HEADS OF BIBB OR BOSTON
    LETTUCE
½ SMALL HEAD OF CURLY CHICORY OR
    ESCAROLE
1 MEDIUM CUCUMBER, SLICED
4½ TEASPOONS SHERRY VINEGAR, OR 1
    TABLESPOON WHITE WINE VINEGAR
    AND 1½ TEASPOONS DRY SHERRY

¾ TEASPOON DIJON MUSTARD
1½ TEASPOONS MINCED PARSLEY
⅓ CUP PEANUT OR OLIVE OIL
⅛ TEASPOON SALT
PINCH OF BLACK PEPPER

**1.** Reserve 8 whole leaves of lettuce for garnish. Tear the remaining greens into bite-size pieces and place them in a large bowl with the cucumber slices.

**2.** In a small bowl, combine the vinegar, mustard, and parsley. Add the oil in a slow stream, beating constantly with a whisk. Add the salt and pepper, and beat again briefly.

**3.** Line the sides of a large salad bowl with overlapping lettuce leaves. When ready to serve, toss the greens and cucumber with the dressing and mound in the center of the bowl.

# Marinated Zucchini Salad

SERVES 4

🕐 EXTRA - QUICK

2 CUPS ¼-INCH-THICK ZUCCHINI
    SLICES
½ CUP VEGETABLE OIL
⅓ CUP WHITE WINE VINEGAR
¼ CUP SUGAR
1 LARGE GARLIC CLOVE, MINCED
¾ TEASPOON SALT
¾ TEASPOON CHOPPED FRESH THYME,
    OR ¼ TEASPOON DRIED

¾ TEASPOON CHOPPED FRESH
    MARJORAM, OR ¼ TEASPOON DRIED
¾ TEASPOON CHOPPED FRESH
    ROSEMARY, OR ¼ TEASPOON DRIED
¾ TEASPOON CHOPPED FRESH DILL, OR
    ¼ TEASPOON DRIED
1 LARGE TOMATO, CUT INTO WEDGES
½ CUP BLACK OLIVES, HALVED

**1.** In a medium saucepan, bring 1 quart of water to a boil. Add the zucchini and simmer for 2 minutes, or just until crisp-tender. Drain the zucchini in a colander and pat dry.

**2.** In a small bowl, combine the oil, vinegar, sugar, garlic, salt, thyme, marjoram, rosemary, and dill.

**3.** In a salad bowl, combine the zucchini, tomato, and olives. Pour just enough dressing over the salad to coat lightly and toss gently.

**4.** Cover and refrigerate the zucchini salad until ready to serve.

**Variation:** *This is a simplified method for preparing vegetables "à la Grecque." In the traditional recipe, the vegetables are actually cooked in the dressing. The technique can be used with many other vegetables, such as broccoli or cauliflower florets, julienne (or baby) carrots, or whole green beans. Just blanch each vegetable until crisp-tender before combining it with the dressing.*

# Spinach Salad with Mushrooms and Croutons

SERVES 4

⏱ EXTRA-QUICK

1 POUND FRESH SPINACH, STEMMED AND TORN INTO BITE-SIZE PIECES
½ CUP SCALLIONS, CUT INTO ¼-INCH PIECES
4 TABLESPOONS UNSALTED BUTTER
1 GARLIC CLOVE, MINCED
1 CUP CUBED ITALIAN BREAD
¾ POUND MUSHROOMS, SLICED ⅛ INCH THICK
2 TABLESPOONS FRESH LEMON JUICE
¼ TEASPOON SALT
PINCH OF BLACK PEPPER

**1.** In a large salad bowl, combine the spinach and the scallions. Cover and refrigerate until ready to serve.

**2.** In a medium skillet, warm 2 tablespoons of the butter with the garlic over medium heat. When the foaming subsides, add the bread cubes and sauté, stirring occasionally, about 5 minutes, or until crisp and golden. Transfer the croutons to a paper-towel-lined plate; set aside.

**3.** Add the remaining 2 tablespoons of butter to the skillet and warm over medium heat until melted. Add the mushrooms and sauté, stirring occasionally, for about 7 minutes, or until the liquid has evaporated and the mushrooms are beginning to brown at the edges. Remove the pan from the heat.

**4.** Add the lemon juice, salt, and pepper to the spinach and scallions, and toss to combine. Add the croutons and mushrooms and toss again.

# GREEN SALAD WITH LEMON-MUSTARD VINAIGRETTE

### SERVES 4
### ⏱ EXTRA-QUICK

2 TABLESPOONS FRESH LEMON JUICE

1 TABLESPOON DIJON MUSTARD

1 TABLESPOON SUGAR

PINCH OF BLACK PEPPER

2 TABLESPOONS CHOPPED FRESH DILL,
    OR 2 TEASPOONS DRIED

6 TABLESPOONS OLIVE OIL

6 LARGE MUSHROOMS, SLICED

1 HEAD OF BOSTON LETTUCE, TORN
    INTO BITE-SIZE PIECES

¼ POUND FRESH SPINACH, STEMMED
    AND TORN INTO BITE-SIZE PIECES

1. In the bottom of a salad bowl, whisk together the lemon juice, mustard, sugar, pepper, dill, and olive oil. The mixture will be thick.

2. Add the mushrooms to the vinaigrette and toss to coat. Add the lettuce and spinach to the salad bowl and toss.

**VARIATION:** *For a vinaigrette with a slightly Asian flavor, omit the sugar; replace 1 tablespoon of the olive oil with dark sesame oil, and use chopped fresh cilantro instead of dill. As a finishing touch, sprinkle the salad with a spoonful of toasted sesame seeds.*

# AVOCADO SALAD

SERVES 4

⏱ EXTRA-QUICK

2 TABLESPOONS SAFFLOWER OIL

2 TABLESPOONS OLIVE OIL

1½ TABLESPOONS WHITE WINE
VINEGAR

1 TEASPOON DIJON MUSTARD

½ TEASPOON SALT

¼ TEASPOON BLACK PEPPER

1 HEAD OF BOSTON LETTUCE

2 RIPE AVOCADOS, CUT INTO ¾-INCH
PIECES

1 SMALL CUCUMBER, PEELED AND
THINLY SLICED

1 SMALL BUNCH OF WATERCRESS,
STEMMED AND SEPARATED INTO
SMALL SPRIGS

**1.** In a large bowl, combine the oils, vinegar, mustard, salt, and pepper, whisking until thoroughly blended.

**2.** Line 4 salad bowls with lettuce leaves.

**3.** Add the avocado to the dressing and toss gently to coat. Add the cucumber slices and watercress sprigs and turn into the lettuce-lined bowls.

**KITCHEN NOTE:** *Avocado flesh will darken if it is cut or mashed and left exposed to air, but tossing the avocado with a dressing that's both oily and acidic helps stop this reaction. It's best to make salads shortly before serving, but if you must make them in advance, cover them with plastic wrap and refrigerate until needed.*

# Marinated Tomato and Red Onion Salad

SERVES 4

⏱ EXTRA-QUICK

1 POUND PLUM TOMATOES

4 TABLESPOONS OLIVE OIL

1 TABLESPOON RED WINE VINEGAR

½ TEASPOON SALT

PINCH OF SUGAR

PINCH OF DRY MUSTARD

2 TABLESPOONS MINCED RED ONION
   PLUS 4 THIN SLICES, SEPARATED
   INTO RINGS

8 FRESH BASIL LEAVES, COARSELY
   CHOPPED, OR ½ TEASPOON DRIED
   BASIL

¼ TEASPOON BLACK PEPPER

**1.** In a medium saucepan, bring 1 quart of water to a boil over high heat.

**2.** With a paring knife, make a small incision in the base of each tomato. Plunge the tomatoes into the boiling water for 15 seconds. Transfer the tomatoes to a colander and refresh under cold running water.

**3.** Meanwhile, in a small bowl, combine the oil, vinegar, salt, sugar, and dry mustard, and whisk until blended; set aside.

**4.** When the tomatoes are cool enough to handle, remove the skins and discard. Cut the tomatoes crosswise into ½-inch-thick slices and arrange half of them in a single layer in a shallow glass or ceramic dish. Sprinkle with half of the minced red onion, half of the basil, and half of the pepper. Top with the remaining tomato slices and sprinkle with the remaining minced onion, basil, and pepper. Top the tomatoes with the onion rings.

**5.** Whisk the dressing to recombine and pour over the salad. Set the salad aside to marinate for at least 15 minutes at room temperature.

# ROMAINE SALAD WITH CUCUMBER-YOGURT DRESSING

SERVES 4

🕐 EXTRA-QUICK

1 SMALL CUCUMBER, PEELED AND
  GRATED
1 TEASPOON SALT
½ CUP PLAIN YOGURT
1 GARLIC CLOVE, MINCED

2 TABLESPOONS OLIVE OIL
PINCH OF BLACK PEPPER
1 SMALL HEAD OF ROMAINE LETTUCE,
  TORN INTO BITE-SIZE PIECES

**1.** Place the grated cucumber in a strainer, sprinkle with the salt, and set aside to drain at least 20 minutes.

**2.** After draining, combine the cucumber, yogurt, garlic, oil, and pepper in a small bowl.

**3.** In a salad bowl, toss the lettuce with the radishes. Add the dressing and toss.

**VARIATION:** *The dressing for this salad resembles the Indian condiment called raita. To serve the dressing as an accompaniment to curries and other Indian dishes, double the recipe, omit the oil, and add ¼ teaspoon each of ground cumin and ground coriander, as well as a pinch of ground red pepper.*

# Tossed Salad with Parmesan Dressing

### SERVES 4
### ⏱ EXTRA-QUICK

4 CUPS OF MIXED SALAD GREENS

6 RED RADISHES, THINLY SLICED

1 SMALL YELLOW BELL PEPPER, CUT INTO THIN STRIPS

1 SMALL GREEN BELL PEPPER, CUT INTO THIN STRIPS

½ CUP ALFALFA SPROUTS

6 OUNCES MUSHROOMS, SLICED

1 SMALL RED ONION, SLICED AND SEPARATED INTO RINGS

¼ CUP GRATED PARMESAN CHEESE

½ CUP OLIVE OIL

2 TABLESPOONS MAYONNAISE

¼ CUP BALSAMIC OR RED WINE VINEGAR

1 GARLIC CLOVE, PEELED

2 TABLESPOONS MINCED CHIVES OR SCALLION GREENS

¼ TEASPOON OREGANO

½ TEASPOON SALT

**1.** In a large salad bowl, combine the greens, radishes, peppers, sprouts, mushrooms, and onions. Cover and refrigerate until ready to serve.

**2.** In a food processor or blender, combine the Parmesan, oil, mayonnaise, vinegar, gar-lic, chives, oregano, and salt and process until smooth. Transfer to a small bowl, cover, and set aside.

**3.** When ready to serve, whisk the dressing briefly to recombine and pour over the salad. Toss until evenly coated.

# Green Bean, Red Onion, and Bacon Salad

SERVES 4

⏲ EXTRA-QUICK

1 POUND GREEN BEANS

4 SLICES BACON, COARSELY CHOPPED

3 TABLESPOONS WHITE OR RED WINE
    VINEGAR

3 TABLESPOONS OLIVE OIL

¼ TEASPOON SALT

PINCH OF BLACK PEPPER

1 SMALL RED ONION, SLICED AND
    SEPARATED INTO RINGS

**1.** In a medium saucepan, bring 2 quarts of water to a boil over high heat. Add the beans to the boiling water, lower the heat to medium, cover, and cook 5 minutes, or until crisp-tender. Drain the beans and transfer them to a large bowl.

**2.** In a small skillet, cook the bacon over medium heat, stirring occasionally, for 5 minutes, or until crisp. Remove the skillet from

the heat and pour off the bacon fat. Add the vinegar, stir, and return to the heat for 1 minute.

**3.** Pour the bacon and vinegar mixture over the beans. Add the oil, salt, and pepper and toss to combine. Arrange the salad on a serving platter and top with the onion rings. Set aside until ready to serve.

**Variation:** *This side dish could easily be turned into a light main dish by adding chunks of turkey, ham, or tuna. If you have some leftover boiled potatoes, toss them with the dressing, too. Serve the salad with crusty whole-wheat rolls.*

# RED AND GREEN CABBAGE SALAD

SERVES 8

4 CUPS SHREDDED RED CABBAGE

4 CUPS SHREDDED GREEN CABBAGE

1 TABLESPOON CHOPPED SCALLIONS

½ CUP RED WINE VINEGAR

1 TABLESPOON SUGAR

1 TEASPOON SALT

1 TEASPOON CARAWAY SEEDS

**1.** Bring 1½ cups water to a boil in a large saucepan over high heat. Drop the shredded cabbage into the boiling water and blanch for 1 minute. Turn the cabbage into a colander to drain.

**2.** In a food processor or blender, combine the scallions, vinegar, sugar, and salt. Process about 20 seconds, or until mixed.

**3.** Transfer the cabbage to a large bowl. Pour the dressing over the cabbage, sprinkle with the caraway seeds, and toss to combine. Cover with plastic wrap and refrigerate for several hours or overnight.

# Cucumber Salad with Sour Cream

SERVES 4

EXTRA-QUICK

2 LARGE CUCUMBERS

2 TEASPOONS SALT

2 MEDIUM ONIONS, PEELED AND
  THINLY SLICED

1 TABLESPOON FRESH LEMON JUICE

⅔ CUP SOUR CREAM

PINCH OF BLACK PEPPER

LARGE OUTER LEAVES OF BIBB OR
  BOSTON LETTUCE

**1.** Peel the cucumbers and slice in half lengthwise. Scoop out the central seedy portions with a spoon and discard, then slice the cucumbers thinly.

**2.** Place the cucumber slices in a small bowl and sprinkle with salt to draw out the excess liquid. Mix well.

**3.** Place the onions in a separate bowl of cold water, then place both bowls in the freezer for 10 minutes.

**4.** Squeeze the cucumber slices by handfuls until they are as dry as possible. Drain the onions and pat them dry.

**5.** In a small bowl, stir the lemon juice into the sour cream. Add the black pepper. Stir in the cucumber and onion and taste for seasoning. Add salt if necessary. Chill the salad until ready to serve.

**6.** Line a serving dish with the lettuce leaves and spoon the cucumber salad on top.

**SUBSTITUTION:** *Use yogurt instead of sour cream to cut calories from this classic salad. Substitute plain low-fat yogurt straight from the carton, or thicken the yogurt first by spooning it into a strainer lined with cheesecloth, then placing it over a bowl and letting it stand for at least an hour. Some of the whey will drain off, leaving the yogurt with a sour cream-like texture. You can make this substitution in just about any dressing or dip that calls for sour cream.*

# GREEK SALAD

SERVES 4

EXTRA-QUICK

1 HEAD OF BOSTON LETTUCE

1 SMALL CUCUMBER, THINLY SLICED

1 MEDIUM TOMATO, CUT INTO WEDGES

1 MEDIUM GREEN BELL PEPPER, CUT INTO ¼-INCH-THICK RINGS

1 SMALL ONION, THINLY SLICED

12 GREEK OLIVES

¼ POUND FETA OR MOZZARELLA CHEESE, CUT INTO 1-INCH CUBES

1 TABLESPOON MINCED FRESH OREGANO, OR 1 TEASPOON DRIED

¼ CUP OLIVE OIL

2 TABLESPOONS RED WINE VINEGAR

2 TEASPOONS SUGAR

½ TEASPOON SALT

**1.** Line a salad bowl with the lettuce leaves. Top with the cucumber, tomato, bell pepper, onion, and olives. Top with the cheese and sprinkle with the oregano. Cover the bowl with plastic wrap and refrigerate until ready to serve.

**2.** Meanwhile, combine the oil, vinegar, sugar, and salt in a jar with a tight-fitting lid. Shake the jar until the dressing is well blended; set aside.

**3.** Just before serving, shake the dressing to recombine and pour over the salad.

# VEGETABLE-PARMESAN SALAD

SERVES 8 TO 10

1 CUP MAYONNAISE

¼ CUP GRATED PARMESAN CHEESE

⅛ CUP SUGAR

½ TEASPOON BASIL

½ TEASPOON SALT

2 CUPS BROCCOLI, CUT INTO BITE-SIZE PIECES

2 CUPS CAULIFLOWER, CUT INTO BITE-SIZE PIECES

1 SMALL RED ONION, SLICED

**1.** In a large bowl, combine the mayonnaise, Parmesan, sugar, basil, and salt. Add the broccoli, cauliflower, and onion and toss to coat.

**2.** Cover and refrigerate the salad for several hours or overnight.

**VARIATION:** *If raw broccoli and cauliflower don't agree with you, just blanch the vegetables instead of using them raw. You can cook the cauliflower and broccoli together: Blanch them for just 1 to 2 minutes in a big pot of boiling water, then rinse them under cold running water to stop the cooking and cool them. Drain well.*

# Carrot, Apple, and Walnut Salad

SERVES 4

⏲ EXTRA-QUICK

1 POUND CARROTS, SHREDDED

2 MEDIUM CRISP RED APPLES, CUT
  INTO THIN SLICES

1 TEASPOON SUGAR

1 TEASPOON GROUND CORIANDER

¾ TEASPOON SALT

¼ CUP CIDER VINEGAR

2 TABLESPOONS CORN OIL

¼ CUP WALNUT PIECES, COARSELY
  CHOPPED

**1.** Combine the carrots and apples in a large bowl.

**2.** In a small bowl, blend the sugar, coriander, salt, vinegar, and oil. Pour the dressing over the carrots and apples, and toss until evenly coated. Cover the bowl and chill until serving time.

**3.** Just before serving, add the walnuts to the bowl and toss to combine. Divide the salad among 4 bowls and serve.

# Spinach and Bacon Salad

SERVES 6

⏱ EXTRA-QUICK

1 CUP OLIVE OIL

¼ CUP CHOPPED PARSLEY

2 GARLIC CLOVES, MINCED

1 TEASPOON BLACK PEPPER

6 SLICES FIRM WHOLE-WHEAT BREAD,
   CUT INTO CUBES

¼ POUND BACON

½ POUND FRESH SPINACH, STEMMED

1 LARGE TOMATO, CUT INTO WEDGES

1 RED ONION, THINLY SLICED

⅓ CUP FRESH LEMON JUICE

4 TEASPOONS DIJON MUSTARD

½ TEASPOON SALT

3 HARD-COOKED EGGS, COARSELY
   CHOPPED

**1.** Preheat the oven to 375°. Line a baking sheet with foil.

**2.** In a medium bowl, stir together ½ cup of the oil, the parsley, garlic, and ½ teaspoon of the pepper. Add the bread cubes and toss until well coated.

**3.** Spread the bread cubes in an even layer on the prepared baking sheet and bake for 15 to 20 minutes, or until golden.

**4.** Meanwhile, in a medium skillet, cook the bacon over medium heat until crisp, about 10 minutes. Drain the bacon on paper towels; crumble and set aside.

**5.** Tear the spinach into bite-size pieces and place in a large salad bowl. Add the tomato and onion to the spinach; set aside.

**6.** In a small bowl, whisk together the remaining ½ cup of oil, the lemon juice, mustard, salt, and the remaining ½ teaspoon pepper.

**7.** Just before serving, add the chopped eggs, crumbled bacon, and croutons to the salad and toss well. Pour the dressing over the salad and serve.

72

# Marinated Mushroom Salad

SERVES 4

EXTRA-QUICK

1 POUND MUSHROOMS, SLICED
1 CUP CHOPPED CELERY
3 TABLESPOONS CHOPPED SCALLIONS
1 TEASPOON DRY MUSTARD
⅛ TEASPOON SALT

PINCH OF BLACK PEPPER
3 TABLESPOONS WHITE WINE VINEGAR
⅓ CUP OLIVE OIL
8 ROMAINE LETTUCE LEAVES

**1.** In a medium bowl, combine the mushrooms, celery, scallions, dry mustard, salt, pepper, vinegar, and olive oil. Marinate in the refrigerator for 30 minutes, or until time to serve.

**2.** Line a medium salad bowl with the lettuce leaves and spoon the mushroom salad into the middle.

**Variation:** *Enhance this Italian-style salad with 2 other favorite Italian ingredients: artichoke hearts and Parmesan. Add the contents of a small jar of marinated artichoke hearts (rinsed and drained) to the salad, and top each portion with broad Parmesan shavings you make with a swivel-bladed vegetable peeler.*

# Marinated Corn Salad

SERVES 8 TO 10

Two 10-ounce packages frozen
   corn, thawed
2 medium zucchini, diced
1 large red bell pepper, diced
1 medium onion, chopped
½ cup olive oil

¼ cup fresh lime juice
2 tablespoons cider vinegar
2 teaspoons cumin
1 teaspoon salt
¼ teaspoon black pepper

**1.** In a large bowl, combine the corn, zucchini, red pepper, and onion.

**2.** In a jar with a tight-fitting lid, combine the oil, lime juice, vinegar, cumin, salt, and pepper. Shake the jar until the dressing is well combined.

**3.** Pour the dressing over the salad, cover, and chill for several hours or overnight. Take the salad out of the refrigerator 30 minutes before serving.

**Kitchen Note:** *If you've never tried making salad dressing by shaking it in a jar, you've just discovered a wonderful kitchen secret that works for any sort of vinaigrette. A mustard jar is the perfect size. And if you end up with leftover dressing, it's all ready to go into the refrigerator for the next time.*

# DESSERTS

# APPLE CRUMB PIE

SERVES 8

1¾ CUPS FLOUR

1 TEASPOON SALT

3 STICKS COLD, UNSALTED BUTTER

2 TO 3 TABLESPOONS COLD WATER

2 POUNDS TART APPLES, CUT INTO ½-
INCH-WIDE WEDGES

2 TABLESPOONS FRESH LEMON JUICE

1 CUP DARK BROWN SUGAR

½ TEASPOON NUTMEG

½ TEASPOON CINNAMON

**1.** Preheat the oven to 350°.

**2.** In a small bowl, combine 1 cup of the flour with ½ teaspoon of the salt.

**3.** Place butter on a cutting board. With a chef's knife, cut the sticks of butter lengthwise in half and then in half again. Keeping the quarters in stick form, make 8 crosswise slices through each stick, so it is divided into 32 cubes. Separate the cubes.

**4.** In a medium bowl, combine 1 stick of the cubed butter with the flour and salt mixture. With a pastry blender or 2 knives, cut the butter into the flour until the mixture resembles coarse meal. Add 2 to 3 tablespoons of cold water, or just enough to make the mixture cohere without becoming too sticky. Form the mixture into a ball.

**5.** Lightly flour a rolling surface and rolling pin. Roll the dough out into a circle large enough to fit a 9-inch pie plate. Gently fold the dough in half and then into quarters. Carefully transfer the dough to the pie plate and unfold, lining the plate.

**6.** In a large mixing bowl, toss the apples with the lemon juice. Arrange the apples in the crust-lined pie plate.

**7.** Wipe out the mixing bowl and in it combine the remaining flour and salt and the brown sugar. Add the remaining 2 sticks of cubed butter to the bowl. With a pastry blender or 2 knives, cut the butter into the dry ingredients until it is crumbly and well combined.

**8.** Sprinkle the apples with the nutmeg and cinnamon, and then the crumb mixture. Bake the pie for 45 minutes.

# DEEP DISH PEAR PIE

SERVES 8

1½ CUPS PLUS 2 TABLESPOONS FLOUR

¾ TEASPOON SALT

⅓ CUP VEGETABLE SHORTENING, CHILLED

4 TABLESPOONS COLD UNSALTED BUTTER

¼ CUP ICE WATER

2½ POUNDS MEDIUM-RIPE PEARS

½ TO 1 CUP MAPLE SYRUP

¼ TEASPOON NUTMEG

¼ TEASPOON CINNAMON

1 TABLESPOON MILK

1 TABLESPOON SUGAR

**1.** Preheat the oven to 425°.

**2.** In a large bowl, combine 1½ cups of the flour and ½ teaspoon of the salt. Using a pastry blender or 2 knives, cut in the shortening and 2 tablespoons of the butter until the mixture resembles coarse cornmeal.

**3.** Sprinkle the ice water over the mixture and stir with a fork until the dough forms a ball and pulls away from the sides of the bowl. Cover the bowl and refrigerate.

**4.** Peel, halve, and core the pears. Cut the pears crosswise into ½-inch-thick slices and place them in a large bowl.

**5.** Blend the remaining flour with 1 tablespoon of butter and add it in bits to the pears.

Add the maple syrup to taste, the remaining salt, nutmeg, and cinnamon; stir to mix. Pour the filling into a deep 9-inch pie plate. Dot with the remaining tablespoon of butter.

**6.** On a floured board, roll out the pastry to the size of the pie plate plus ½ inch. Cover the pears with the pastry and turn under the overhanging edge. Flute the edge of the crust and cut several steam vents on top. Brush the pastry with the milk and sprinkle with the sugar.

**7.** Bake the pie on the middle rack of the oven for 30 to 45 minutes, or until the crust is golden brown and the filling is bubbling. Serve warm.

# CHOCOLATE CHIP-ALMOND POUND CAKE

SERVES 16

1½ CUPS SLICED ALMONDS
3 CUPS FLOUR
1 TEASPOON BAKING POWDER
¼ TEASPOON SALT
3 STICKS BUTTER, AT ROOM
    TEMPERATURE

2 CUPS SUGAR
8 EGGS
1½ TEASPOONS ALMOND EXTRACT
ONE 6-OUNCE PACKAGE SEMISWEET
    CHOCOLATE CHIPS

**1.** Preheat the oven to 350°. Butter and flour a 10-inch Bundt or other fluted tube pan.

**2.** In a large nonstick skillet, toast the almonds over medium heat, stirring frequently so that they toast evenly, about 10 minutes. Remove the almonds from the pan to cool while you mix the batter.

**3.** In a medium bowl, combine the flour, baking powder, and salt, and thoroughly blend.

**4.** In a mixing bowl, cream the butter and sugar. Beat the eggs in one at a time, beating well after each addition. Beat in the almond extract.

**5.** Beat in the dry ingredients. By hand, stir in the chocolate chips and the cooled toasted almonds.

**6.** Turn the batter into the prepared pan and spread it evenly. Rap the pan on the counter once or twice to remove any air pockets.

**7.** Bake the cake for 1 hour and 5 minutes, or until a toothpick inserted halfway between the tube and the edge of the pan comes out clean.

**8.** Cool the cake in the pan on a rack for about 30 minutes. Unmold the cake onto the rack and let cool completely.

# STRAWBERRY CHEESECAKE PIE

SERVES 8

TWO 8-OUNCE PACKAGES CREAM
CHEESE, AT ROOM TEMPERATURE
½ CUP SUGAR
1 EGG
1 CUP SOUR CREAM
1½ TEASPOONS GRATED LEMON ZEST
1 TABLESPOON FRESH LEMON JUICE

1 TEASPOON VANILLA EXTRACT
ONE 8-INCH GRAHAM CRACKER CRUST,
STORE-BOUGHT OR HOMEMADE
1 CUP HALVED STRAWBERRIES
2 TABLESPOONS RED CURRANT OR
STRAWBERRY JELLY

**1.** Preheat the oven to 350°.

**2.** In a food processor, beat the cream cheese until smooth. Beat in the sugar and egg. Beat in the sour cream, lemon zest, lemon juice, and vanilla.

**3.** Pour the mixture into the graham cracker crust and bake for 35 minutes, or until set.

**4.** Place the pie on a rack to cool to room temperature and then chill for at least 1 hour.

**5.** Before serving, arrange the strawberries around the top edge of the cheesecake pie.

**6.** Melt the jelly in a small saucepan, or in the microwave, and spoon or brush the melted jelly over the strawberries to glaze them.

**Variation:** *Raspberries are pricey (unless they grow in your back yard), but they certainly add an air of luxury to desserts for special occasions. You could edge the cake with fresh raspberries, or, if you really have a bounty of berries, "pave" the whole top with them. Use raspberry jelly for the glaze.*

# CRANBERRY-APPLE PANDOWDY

SERVES 6

♡ LOW-FAT

1 GRANNY SMITH APPLE, CUT INTO
½-INCH CUBES

1 POUND CRANBERRIES, FRESH OR
FROZEN

½ CUP GOLDEN RAISINS

½ CUP PLUS 2 TABLESPOONS DARK
BROWN SUGAR

1½ TEASPOONS ALMOND EXTRACT

1 EGG

¼ CUP PLAIN YOGURT

3 TABLESPOONS BUTTER, MELTED

⅔ CUP FLOUR

½ TEASPOON BAKING POWDER

PINCH OF SALT

**1.** Preheat the oven to 375°. Butter a shallow 1½-quart baking dish.

**2.** In a medium bowl, stir together the apple, cranberries, raisins, ½ cup of the brown sugar, and the almond extract. Pour the fruit mixture into the prepared baking dish.

**3.** In another medium bowl, beat the egg with the yogurt and melted butter. Stir in the flour, the remaining 2 tablespoons brown sugar, the baking powder, and salt.

**4.** Spread the batter evenly over the fruit mixture and bake for 30 to 35 minutes, or until the topping is light golden brown.

**5.** Serve the pandowdy warm, or at room temperature.

**KITCHEN NOTE:** *As its name suggests, a pandowdy is a down-to-earth dessert: not as prim and pretty as a lattice-topped pie, but just as delicious. To serve the pandowdy, cut the crust into 6 wedges, then divide the filling among 6 dessert plates. Top each portion with some of the crust, or spoon the fruit over the wedges of crust.*

# TENNESSEE BLACK CAKE

SERVES 8

2 TEASPOONS COCOA POWDER
3 STICKS UNSALTED BUTTER
EIGHT 1-OUNCE SQUARES
    UNSWEETENED CHOCOLATE
2½ CUPS ALL-PURPOSE FLOUR
¼ TEASPOON PLUS A PINCH OF SALT
2 CUPS SUGAR

2 TEASPOONS BAKING SODA
4 LARGE EGGS
1 CUP BUTTERMILK
3 TEASPOONS VANILLA EXTRACT
½ CUP EVAPORATED MILK
1 POUND POWDERED SUGAR

**1.** Preheat the oven to 350°. Lightly grease two 8½-inch round baking pans and dust each with 1 teaspoon of the cocoa powder.

**2.** Cut 2 sticks of the butter into 8 pieces each. Combine the butter with 4 squares of the chocolate in the top of a double boiler set over, not in, barely simmering water and stir until melted, 1 to 2 minutes. Remove the chocolate from the heat and set aside to cool.

**3.** In a medium bowl, combine the flour, ¼ teaspoon of salt, the sugar, and baking soda. Break the eggs into a large bowl and beat with the buttermilk and 2 teaspoons of the vanilla.

**4.** Gradually add the flour mixture to the egg mixture, stirring until well blended. Slowly pour in the melted chocolate, stirring until smooth. Divide the batter between the pans.

**5.** Place the pans on the middle rack of the oven and bake for 25 to 30 minutes, or until a

toothpick inserted in the center of the cake comes out clean. Be careful not to overbake.

**6.** Cool the cakes in the pans on wire racks, about 10 minutes. Remove the layers from the pans, place on the racks, and allow to cool completely before frosting.

**7.** Cut the remaining stick of butter into 8 pieces. Place the remaining chocolate and butter in the top of a double boiler set over, not in, barely simmering water and stir occasionally until melted, 1 to 2 minutes. Remove the chocolate from the heat and set aside.

**8.** In a medium bowl, combine the milk, powdered sugar, remaining vanilla extract and salt, and the cooled chocolate. Beat the mixture vigorously until the frosting thickens to spreading consistency.

**9.** Frost one layer of the cake. Top with the second layer and frost the top and sides.

# Peanut Butter Cup Pie

SERVES 8

1 STICK PLUS 1 TABLESPOON BUTTER
THIRTY-FIVE 2-INCH GINGERSNAPS
2 TABLESPOONS SUGAR
3 OUNCES SEMISWEET CHOCOLATE
1½ CUPS PEANUT BUTTER

⅓ CUP BROWN SUGAR
1 CUP MILK
½ CUP LIGHT CREAM OR HALF-AND-
  HALF
1 TEASPOON VANILLA EXTRACT

**1.** Melt the stick of butter on the stovetop or in the microwave. Set aside to cool slightly.

**2.** Place the gingersnaps in a food processor or blender and process to form fine crumbs. Turn the crumbs into a bowl. Add the melted butter and the sugar and blend well. Press the crumb mixture evenly into a 9-inch pie plate to form a crust; set aside.

**3.** Place the chocolate and the remaining 1 tablespoon butter in the top of a double boiler set over, not in, barely simmering water and stir occasionally until melted, 1 to 2 minutes. Remove the chocolate from the heat and set aside.

**4.** In a medium bowl, beat the peanut butter until softened and smooth. Gradually beat in the sugar. Add the milk, cream, and vanilla, and continue beating until smooth.

**5.** Pour the peanut-butter filling into the crust. Pour in the melted chocolate mixture, and gently swirl it through the peanut-butter filling; do not blend completely.

**6.** Cover the pie with plastic wrap and place it in the freezer for at least 6 hours, or overnight.

**7.** Let the pie stand at room temperature for 15 minutes before serving.

# BLUEBERRY CRUMBLE

SERVES 8

⏱ EXTRA-QUICK

4 CUPS BLUEBERRIES, FRESH OR FROZEN
1 TABLESPOON FRESH LEMON JUICE
3 TABLESPOONS SUGAR
½ CUP PLUS 3 TABLESPOONS FLOUR
1 TEASPOON ALLSPICE

⅓ CUP ROLLED OATS
⅓ CUP BROWN SUGAR
¼ TEASPOON SALT
⅓ CUP BUTTER
⅔ CUP CHOPPED WALNUTS

**1.** Preheat the oven to 375°. Butter and flour a shallow 1½-quart baking dish.

**2.** In a large bowl, toss the blueberries with the lemon juice, sugar, 3 tablespoons of the flour, and ½ teaspoon of the allspice. Transfer the mixture to the prepared baking dish.

**3.** In a small bowl, combine the remaining ½ cup flour with the oats, brown sugar, salt, and the remaining ½ teaspoon allspice. With a pastry blender or two knives, cut in the butter until the mixture is coarse and crumbly. Stir in the chopped walnuts.

**4.** Sprinkle the walnut topping over the blueberries and bake for 30 minutes, or until the topping begins to brown.

**KITCHEN NOTE:** *A pastry blender is not an electrical appliance, but rather an inexpensive, handy gadget for mixing fat into dry ingredients. It consists of a set of curved wires or tines set into a handle, allowing you to use an efficient one-handed chopping motion to blend the ingredients to the proper crumbly consistency.*

# BUTTER-WALNUT BAKED PEARS AND APPLES

SERVES 4

⏰ EXTRA-QUICK

4 TABLESPOONS BUTTER, AT ROOM
TEMPERATURE
3 TABLESPOONS BROWN SUGAR
1 TEASPOON CINNAMON
½ TEASPOON NUTMEG

¼ CUP FINELY CHOPPED WALNUTS
2 LARGE PEARS, PREFERABLY BARTLETT,
UNPEELED
2 LARGE GRANNY SMITH APPLES,
UNPEELED

**1.** Preheat the oven to 375°. Lightly butter a baking dish big enough to hold the fruit.

**2.** In a small bowl, cream the butter and brown sugar. Beat in the cinnamon and nutmeg. Stir in the walnuts.

**3.** Cut a thin slice off the bottoms of the pears and apples to help them stand upright, if necessary. Core the fruit from the top, making a hole ½ to ¾ inch in diameter, and stopping short of the bottoms.

**4.** Dividing evenly, use a knife to stuff the fruit with the butter-nut mixture.

**5.** Place the fruit in the prepared baking dish and bake for 20 minutes, or until the fruit is just tender.

**VARIATION:** *For a change, fill the pears and apples with a butter-almond mixture. Buy slivered almonds and toast them before chopping them. Add a few drops of almond extract to the butter mixture.*

# ALMOND-FRUIT TART

SERVES 8

⅓ CUP SLICED ALMONDS

1½ CUPS FLOUR

¼ CUP SUGAR

½ TEASPOON SALT

10 TABLESPOONS COLD BUTTER, CUT INTO PIECES

TWO 3-OUNCE PACKAGES CREAM CHEESE, AT ROOM TEMPERATURE

1⅓ CUPS SOUR CREAM

1 TEASPOON ALMOND EXTRACT

3 CUPS MIXED SLICED FRUIT, FRESH OR FROZEN

2 TABLESPOONS STRAWBERRY JELLY

**1.** Preheat the oven to 450°.

**2.** In a food processor, finely chop the almonds (do not overprocess or the almonds will turn into a paste).

**3.** Add the flour, 3 tablespoons of the sugar, and the salt and process to blend. Add the butter and pulse until the dough just holds together.

**4.** Press the dough evenly into the bottom and up the sides of a 9-inch tart pan with a removable bottom. Bake the tart shell for 5 minutes (the dough will puff slightly). Remove the tart shell from the oven but leave the oven on.

**5.** Meanwhile, in the same processor work bowl, blend the cream cheese, sour cream, almond extract and the remaining sugar.

**6.** Spread the cream cheese mixture evenly in the tart shell and return to the oven. Bake for 7 to 9 minutes, or until set. Set the tart aside on a rack to cool.

**7.** If using fresh fruit, slice it and toss with some lemon juice to keep it from discoloring. If using frozen fruit, drain the thawed fruit well on paper towels. Arrange the fruit on top of the cooled pie.

**8.** In a small saucepan over low heat, or in the microwave, melt the strawberry jelly. Spoon or brush the jelly over the fruit.

# STRAWBERRY-APRICOT SHORTCAKE

SERVES 6

2 CUPS FLOUR

⅓ CUP SUGAR

1 TABLESPOON BAKING POWDER

½ TEASPOON SALT

1 STICK COLD BUTTER, CUT INTO
  PIECES

1¼ CUPS HEAVY CREAM

½ CUP APRICOT PRESERVES

1 PINT STRAWBERRIES, HALVED

1 TABLESPOON POWDERED SUGAR

WHOLE STRAWBERRIES, FOR GARNISH
  (OPTIONAL)

**1.** Preheat the oven to 450°. Lightly butter a baking sheet.

**2.** In a large bowl, combine the flour, sugar, baking powder, and salt. With a pastry blender or 2 knives, cut in the butter until the mixture resembles coarse meal.

**3.** Pour in ¾ cup of the cream and blend until a soft dough is formed. Transfer the dough to a lightly floured surface and knead it for about 1 minute, adding a tablespoon or two of flour, if necessary, to keep the dough from sticking.

**4.** Roll the dough into a circle about ½ inch thick. With a floured plain or scalloped 3-inch round cutter, cut out 6 rounds (you may need to gather the scraps and reroll the dough to get all 6 shortcakes).

**5.** Bake the shortcakes on the prepared baking sheet for 10 to 12 minutes, or until golden brown. Cool them on a rack.

**6.** Meanwhile, in a small saucepan, stir the apricot preserves over medium-low heat until melted, about 5 minutes. Place the strawberry halves in a bowl, pour the melted preserves on top, and toss the fruit gently to mix.

**7.** In a small mixing bowl, beat the remaining ½ cup heavy cream with the powdered sugar until stiff peaks form.

**8.** To serve, split the shortcakes in half. Cover the bottom half with the strawberry-apricot mixture and replace the top. Serve with the sweetened whipped cream and garnish with whole strawberries, if desired.

# RICE PUDDING WITH DRIED FRUIT

SERVES 6

1½ CUPS LIGHT CREAM OR HALF-AND-HALF

1½ CUPS HEAVY CREAM

⅓ CUP MAPLE SYRUP

3 EGGS

3 EGG YOLKS

¾ TEASPOON VANILLA EXTRACT

½ TEASPOON NUTMEG

1 CUP MIXED DRIED FRUIT, CHOPPED

½ CUP GOLDEN RAISINS

2 CUPS RICE

**1.** Preheat the oven to 325°. Butter a shallow 1-quart baking dish.

**2.** In a large bowl, whisk together the light cream, heavy cream, maple syrup, eggs, egg yolks, vanilla, and nutmeg. Stir in the dried fruit, raisins, and rice.

**3.** Turn the mixture into the prepared dish and bake, uncovered, for 35 minutes.

**4.** Stir the mixture in the baking dish and bake for an additional 5 minutes, or until the custard is set. Serve warm or chilled.

**KITCHEN NOTE:** *Maple syrup is not just another sweetener; it has an inimitable flavor that can't be matched by supermarket "pancake syrups." Pure maple syrup is sold in several grades: The darker grade "B," which has a stronger flavor than table-grade syrup, is fine for cooking. Once the bottle or tin has been opened, store maple syrup in the refrigerator.*

# KEY LIME PIE

SERVES 8

11 GRAHAM CRACKERS
2 TABLESPOONS SUGAR
6 TABLESPOONS BUTTER, MELTED
3 EGGS
3 EGG YOLKS
ONE 14-OUNCE CAN SWEETENED
    CONDENSED MILK

⅔ CUP FRESH LIME JUICE
1 TABLESPOON GRATED LIME ZEST
UNSWEETENED WHIPPED CREAM, FOR
    GARNISH (OPTIONAL)

**1.** Preheat the oven to 375°.

**2.** In a food processor or blender, process the crackers and sugar until the crackers form fine crumbs. Turn the crumb mixture into a bowl, add the melted butter, and blend well.

**3.** Press the crumb mixture into a 9-inch pie plate to form a crust. Bake for 8 to 10 minutes, or until the crust just begins to color. Let the crust cool before filling it.

**4.** Lower the oven temperature to 350°.

**5.** In a large bowl, beat the eggs and egg yolks together. Whisk in the sweetened condensed milk. Stir in the lime juice and zest.

**6.** Gently pour the filling into the cooled crust and bake for 10 to 12 minutes, or until just set. Let the pie cool to room temperature and then refrigerate until chilled, 4 to 6 hours. Serve with the unsweetened whipped cream, if desired.

# ⊙ OPEN-FACED PEACH PIE

SERVES 8

1¼ CUPS FLOUR

2 TABLESPOONS SUGAR

¾ TEASPOON SALT

4 TABLESPOONS COLD BUTTER, CUT
    INTO PIECES

3 TABLESPOONS VEGETABLE
    SHORTENING, CHILLED AND CUT
    INTO PIECES

4 TO 5 TABLESPOONS ICE WATER

8 TO 10 RIPE PEACHES, CUT INTO
    ½-INCH-THICK SLICES

1 TABLESPOON FRESH LEMON JUICE

½ CUP SUGAR

5 TABLESPOONS CORNSTARCH

2 TEASPOONS GRATED ORANGE ZEST

¾ TEASPOON CINNAMON

**1.** In a large bowl, combine the flour, sugar, and ½ teaspoon of the salt. With a pastry blender or 2 knives, cut in the butter and shortening until the mixture resembles coarse crumbs.

**2.** Sprinkle 2 tablespoons of the ice water over the mixture and toss it with a fork. The dough should be just barely moistened, enough so it will hold together when it is formed into a ball. If necessary, add up to 3 tablespoons of water, 1 tablespoon at a time. Form the dough into a flat disc, wrap in plastic wrap, and refrigerate for 30 minutes.

**3.** On a lightly floured surface, roll out the dough to a 12-inch circle. Fit the dough into a 9-inch glass pie plate. Trim the overhang to an even ½ inch all the way around. Fold the overhang under and crimp the dough to form a decorative border. Prick the pastry with a fork. Place the pie shell in the freezer to chill for at least 15 minutes before baking.

**4.** Preheat the oven to 425°.

**5.** Place the peaches in a large bowl; add the lemon juice and toss to coat. Add the sugar, cornstarch, orange zest, cinnamon, and remaining salt, and toss until well mixed.

**6.** Spoon the filling into the shell and bake for 35 to 40 minutes, or until the crust is golden. Cool the pie slightly before serving.

# BLUEBERRY-CHERRY COBBLER

SERVES 8

2 CUPS FLOUR

¼ CUP PLUS 2 TABLESPOONS SUGAR

2 TEASPOONS BAKING POWDER

½ TEASPOON SALT

7 TABLESPOONS COLD BUTTER—4 CUT
INTO PIECES AND 3 MELTED

½ CUP MILK

ONE 17-OUNCE CAN DARK SWEET
PITTED CHERRIES

2 TABLESPOONS CORNSTARCH

2½ CUPS FRESH BLUEBERRIES

2 TEASPOONS GRATED LEMON ZEST

**1.** Preheat the oven to 425°.

**2.** In a large bowl, combine the flour, ¼ cup of sugar, the baking powder, and salt. With a pastry blender or 2 knives, cut the pieces of butter into the dry ingredients until the mixture resembles coarse meal. Gradually pour in the milk and mix until a soft dough forms.

**3.** Transfer the dough to a lightly floured surface and knead gently several times. Roll the dough into a circle about ½ inch thick. With a floured 2½-inch round cookie cutter, cut out 8 rounds and set aside.

**4.** Reserving ⅓ cup of the liquid, drain the cherries. In a large bowl, combine the reserved cherry liquid, the melted butter, the remaining sugar, and the cornstarch. Stir in the cherries, blueberries, and lemon zest.

**5.** Spread the filling evenly in an 8- x 10- x 2-inch baking dish. Place the circles of dough on top. Bake for 25 minutes, or until the topping is golden.

**KITCHEN NOTE:** *Because blueberries are commercially frozen without sugar or syrup, they can almost always be substituted for fresh berries. You can also freeze blueberries yourself: Spread unwashed berries in a shallow pan and freeze until they're rock-hard, then transfer them to zip-seal bags. Rinse and pat dry before using.*

# New Orleans Bread Pudding with Bourbon Sauce

SERVES 8

1 STICK BUTTER

1½ CUPS PECANS, TOASTED AND CHOPPED

1 CUP LIGHT BROWN SUGAR

2 TEASPOONS VANILLA EXTRACT

1½ TEASPOONS CINNAMON

5 EGGS

2 CUPS MILK

1 CUP GOLDEN RAISINS

12 SLICES DAY-OLD FIRM-TEXTURED WHITE BREAD, CUT INTO CUBES

⅓ CUP DARK BROWN SUGAR

½ TEASPOON NUTMEG

1 TEASPOON CORNSTARCH

¼ CUP HEAVY CREAM

2 TABLESPOONS BOURBON

**1.** Preheat the oven to 350°. Butter an 8-inch square baking pan.

**2.** Melt 4 tablespoons of the butter on the stovetop or in the microwave. In a small bowl, combine the melted butter, 1 cup of the pecans, ½ cup of the light brown sugar, 1 teaspoon of the vanilla, and 1 teaspoon of the cinnamon. In a large bowl, beat the eggs until frothy. Add the pecan mixture and blend well. Stir in the milk and raisins.

**3.** Place the bread cubes in the prepared pan. Pour the egg mixture over them and toss gently until the bread is soaked. Let the pudding sit until the bread has absorbed nearly all of the liquid, about 35 minutes. Stir the mixture once or twice to moisten the bread evenly.

**4.** Meanwhile, in a small bowl, combine the remaining pecans, the dark brown sugar, nutmeg, and the remaining cinnamon. Set aside.

**5.** Bake the pudding for 25 minutes. Sprinkle the pecan-sugar mixture over the pudding and continue baking for 10 minutes, or until the pudding is set and the topping browned.

**6.** Meanwhile, in a small saucepan, warm the remaining butter with the remaining light brown sugar and cornstarch over medium heat until the sugar is dissolved. Whisk in the cream and the remaining vanilla and cook, stirring, until the sauce thickens slightly, 1 to 2 minutes. Stir in the bourbon and cook, stirring, for another 30 seconds. Remove the sauce from the heat and let it cool slightly.

**7.** Serve the pudding with the sauce spooned over the top.

# One-Pan Chocolate Walnut Cake

SERVES 10

🕐 EXTRA-QUICK

1 CUP FLOUR

1 CUP SUGAR

⅔ CUP COCOA POWDER

1 TEASPOON BAKING POWDER

½ TEASPOON BAKING SODA

½ CUP SOUR CREAM

¼ CUP VEGETABLE OIL

3 EGGS

1 TEASPOON VANILLA EXTRACT

1 CUP CHOPPED WALNUTS

**1.** Preheat the oven to 350°. Butter and flour an 8-inch square or round cake pan, preferably nonstick.

**2.** In the prepared baking pan, combine the flour, sugar, cocoa, baking powder, and baking soda and stir to blend thoroughly. Make a well in the center of the dry ingredients.

**3.** Place the sour cream, oil, eggs, and vanilla in the well. With a fork or small whisk, lightly beat the wet ingredients together.

**4.** Gradually incorporate all of the dry ingredients into the wet ingredients by pulling the dry ingredients in from the edges as you stir. Stir in the walnuts.

**5.** Spread the mixture evenly in the pan and rap it once or twice on the counter to remove any air bubbles in the batter.

**6.** Bake for 25 to 30 minutes, or until a toothpick inserted in the center comes out clean. Cool the cake in the pan on a rack.

# SHOOFLY PIE

SERVES 8

1 CUP FLOUR

1 CUP DARK BROWN SUGAR

½ TEASPOON CINNAMON

½ TEASPOON NUTMEG

3 TABLESPOONS COLD BUTTER, CUT
INTO PIECES

1 EGG

¾ CUP LIGHT UNSULPHURED MOLASSES

1 CUP BOILING WATER

1 TEASPOON BAKING SODA

ONE 9-INCH PIE CRUST, STORE-
BOUGHT OR HOMEMADE

1. Preheat the oven to 450°.

2. In a large bowl, combine the flour, sugar, cinnamon, and nutmeg. With a pastry blender or two knives, cut in the butter until the mixture resembles coarse crumbs. (Don't worry if the dry ingredients do not appear to be completely incorporated at this stage.)

3. In a medium bowl, lightly beat the egg. Beat in the molasses; set aside.

4. Pour the boiling water into a heatproof cup and stir in the baking soda. Gradually add the baking soda mixture to the molasses mixture, beating until well incorporated.

5. Stir 1 cup of the crumb mixture into the molasses mixture, and pour it into the pie shell. Sprinkle the remaining crumb mixture evenly over the filling and place the pie in the oven. Reduce the oven temperature to 350° and bake the pie for about 30 minutes, or until the filling is set and puffed and does not quiver when the pie is shaken gently. Serve the pie warm, or at room temperature.

# ⊙ORANGE CARROT CAKE

SERVES 8

3 CUPS FLOUR

2 TEASPOONS BAKING SODA

½ TEASPOON SALT

4 STICKS BUTTER, AT ROOM
TEMPERATURE

1 CUP DARK BROWN SUGAR

⅔ CUP SUGAR

4 EGGS

4 CUPS GRATED CARROTS

1 CUP CHOPPED WALNUTS

1 CUP GOLDEN RAISINS

1 TABLESPOON PLUS 1 TEASPOON
GRATED ORANGE ZEST

2 TEASPOONS VANILLA EXTRACT

11 OUNCES CREAM CHEESE, AT ROOM
TEMPERATURE

2½ CUPS POWDERED SUGAR

**1.** Preheat the oven to 350°. Butter two 8- x 2-inch round cake pans and line the bottoms with circles of wax paper. Butter the wax paper, then flour the pans.

**2.** In a medium bowl, stir together the flour, baking soda, and salt.

**3.** In a large bowl, cream 2 sticks of the butter and the sugars until smoothly blended. Beat in the eggs, one at a time, beating well after each addition, until the batter is thick and light. Add the dry ingredients and beat just until blended; do not overbeat.

**4.** Add the carrots, walnuts, raisins, 1 teaspoon of the orange zest, and 1 teaspoon of the vanilla, and stir until blended.

**5.** Spread the batter evenly in the prepared pans. Rap the pans once or twice on the counter to remove any air pockets. Bake for

35 to 40 minutes, or until the tops are golden, the cakes shrink from the sides of the pans, and a toothpick inserted in the center of the cakes comes out clean.

**6.** Let the cakes cool in the pans for 10 minutes, then turn them out onto a rack to cool completely before frosting.

**7.** Meanwhile, in a medium bowl, beat the cream cheese and the remaining butter until smooth. Beat in the remaining orange zest and the remaining vanilla. Gradually add the powdered sugar, beating well after each addition until the frosting is thick and smooth.

**8.** Remove the wax paper from the cakes. Spread a generous layer of frosting over one cake. Top with the second cake, then frost the top and sides.

# PEAR-APPLE CRISP

SERVES 4

🕐 EXTRA-QUICK

4 MEDIUM GRANNY SMITH APPLES,
    CUT INTO ½-INCH-THICK SLICES
2 FIRM MEDIUM PEARS, CUT INTO
    ⅛-INCH-THICK SLICES
2 CUPS CHOPPED WALNUTS
½ CUP FRESH BREAD CRUMBS

1 CUP DARK BROWN SUGAR
1 TABLESPOON FRESH LEMON JUICE
¾ TEASPOON CINNAMON
⅔ CUP FLOUR
⅓ CUP ROLLED OATS
1 STICK BUTTER, MELTED

**1.** Preheat the oven to 350°. Butter a shallow 1-quart baking dish.

**2.** In a large bowl, toss together the apples, pears, 1 cup of the walnuts, the bread crumbs, ½ cup of the sugar, the lemon juice, and ½ teaspoon of the cinnamon. Turn the mixture into the prepared baking dish.

**3.** In a medium bowl, combine the remaining walnuts, the flour, oats, the remaining sugar, and the remaining cinnamon. Add the melted butter and toss with a fork to evenly distribute.

**4.** Sprinkle the topping over the fruit and bake for 30 minutes, or until the fruit is tender and the topping is browned and crisp.

**KITCHEN NOTE:** *The ever-popular Granny Smith is just one apple option for this recipe. Many apples are more flavorful, though Granny Smiths are reliably firm. Idareds and Empires are two good cooking (and eating) apples that you may find locally in the fall. Visit your local orchard or farm market and ask for recommendations—apple growers tend to be well versed in apple cookery.*

# APPLE CAKE

SERVES 8

3 MEDIUM GRANNY SMITH, OR OTHER
    TART GREEN APPLES, PEELED AND
    FINELY CHOPPED
¼ CUP LEMON JUICE
1 TEASPOON GRATED LEMON ZEST
1½ CUPS FLOUR
1 TEASPOON BAKING SODA
1 TEASPOON CINNAMON
½ TEASPOON NUTMEG

½ TEASPOON SALT
1 STICK BUTTER, AT ROOM
    TEMPERATURE
⅔ CUP DARK BROWN SUGAR
2 EGGS, LIGHTLY BEATEN
1 CUP RAISINS
1 CUP COARSELY CHOPPED WALNUTS
1 TEASPOON VANILLA EXTRACT

**1.** Preheat the oven to 350°. Butter and flour a 9-inch square baking pan.

**2.** Place the apples in a medium bowl, add the lemon juice and zest, and toss well to coat the apples; set aside.

**3.** In a small bowl, stir together the flour, baking soda, cinnamon, nutmeg, and salt; set aside.

**4.** In a large bowl, cream the butter and sugar. Beat in the eggs. Gradually add the dry ingredients, beating well after each addition.

Add the apple mixture, the raisins, walnuts, and vanilla, and stir until well blended.

**5.** Spread the batter evenly in the prepared pan, smoothing the top with a rubber spatula. Rap the pan once or twice on the counter to remove any air pockets. Bake for 45 to 50 minutes, or until the cake shrinks from the sides of the pan and a toothpick inserted in the center of the cake comes out clean.

**6.** Let the cake cool in the pan on a rack, then cut into squares and serve it directly from the pan.

# CHICKEN AND DUMPLINGS

SERVES 4

ONE 3-POUND CHICKEN
4 CUPS CHICKEN BROTH
1 MEDIUM ONION, QUARTERED
2 MEDIUM CARROTS
2 CELERY RIBS
10 SPRIGS OF PARSLEY, PLUS 2
    TABLESPOONS CHOPPED PARSLEY
1 BAY LEAF
1½ CUPS FLOUR

7 TABLESPOONS BUTTER, AT ROOM
    TEMPERATURE
2 TEASPOONS BAKING POWDER
¾ TEASPOON SALT
¼ TEASPOON PEPPER
¼ CUP MILK
1 EGG, LIGHTLY BEATEN
1 CUP CHOPPED SCALLIONS

**1.** In a Dutch oven or heatproof casserole, place the chicken, broth, onion, carrots, celery, parsley sprigs, and bay leaf. Add enough water to cover the chicken. Bring to a boil over medium-high heat. Reduce the heat to medium-low, cover, and simmer until the chicken is tender, about 45 minutes.

**2.** Transfer the chicken to a serving platter and cover with foil to keep warm. Discarding the broth vegetables, skim any fat from the surface, and measure out 6 cups of broth.

**3.** In a small bowl, with your fingertips, thoroughly blend ¼ cup of the flour with 4 tablespoons of the butter. In a large saucepan, bring the 6 cups of broth to a boil over medium-high heat. Pinch off pieces of the flour-butter mixture and drop them, one at a time, into the broth, stirring to incorporate

after each addition. Reduce the heat to medium-low and let the sauce simmer while you make the dumplings.

**4.** In a large bowl, combine the remaining flour with the baking powder, salt, and pepper. Cut in the remaining 3 tablespoons butter until the mixture resembles coarse meal. Stir in the chopped parsley. Add the milk and egg and blend to form a soft dough.

**5.** Increase the heat under the sauce to medium-high and bring to a boil. Drop the dumpling dough, a tablespoonful at a time, into the broth. Reduce the heat to medium-low, cover, and simmer for 10 minutes.

**6.** Just before serving, stir in the scallions. Spoon the dumplings and some of the sauce around the chicken on the serving platter. Pass any remaining sauce separately.

# STOVETOP COUNTRY CAPTAIN

SERVES 4 TO 6

½ CUP SLICED ALMONDS

½ CUP FLOUR

1 TEASPOON SALT

¼ TEASPOON PEPPER

ONE 2½-POUND CHICKEN, CUT INTO 8
    SERVING PIECES

2 TABLESPOONS VEGETABLE OIL

2 TABLESPOONS BUTTER

1 MEDIUM ONION, CHOPPED

2 GARLIC CLOVES, CRUSHED

2 TABLESPOONS CURRY POWDER

½ TEASPOON THYME

TWO 14-OUNCE CANS WHOLE
    TOMATOES

1 CUP RAISINS

¼ CUP CHOPPED PARSLEY

6 CUPS STEAMED RICE

**1.** Preheat the oven to 375°. Place the almonds on an ungreased cookie sheet and toast for 10 minutes, or until golden.

**2.** In a shallow bowl, mix together the flour, ½ teaspoon of the salt, and the pepper. Dredge the chicken in the seasoned flour.

**3.** In a large skillet, warm the oil with the butter over medium-high heat until the butter is melted. Add the chicken and brown well on all sides, 15 to 20 minutes.

**4.** Remove the chicken and set aside. Pour off all but 1 tablespoon of the fat from the skillet.

Add the onion, garlic, curry powder, thyme, and the remaining ½ teaspoon salt to the skillet. Cook over low heat for 5 minutes, stirring to loosen the browned bits clinging to pan.

**5.** Add the tomatoes with their juice, breaking them up with the back of a spoon. Return the chicken, skin-side up, to the skillet, cover, and simmer until the chicken is tender when pierced with a fork, 20 to 30 minutes.

**6.** Stir in the raisins and parsley. Sprinkle the chicken with the toasted almonds and serve hot over the rice.

**KITCHEN NOTE:** *This Southern recipe dates back to the time when clipper ships loaded with spices plied the waters between India and American coastal cities such as Savannah, Georgia. The dish's seasonings certainly hint at Indian origins. Although its ingredients often vary, Country Captain is always served with rice, as befits an Indian-inspired meal.*

# RICE-STUFFED CHICKEN BREASTS

SERVES 4

¼ CUP GOLDEN RAISINS

2 TABLESPOONS MADEIRA

½ CUP LONG-GRAIN WHITE RICE

4 TABLESPOONS PLUS 2 TEASPOONS
  BUTTER

4 OUNCES CHOPPED PECANS

⅓ CUP MINCED SHALLOTS

6 STRIPS ORANGE PEEL, THINLY SLICED

¼ TEASPOON SALT

PINCH OF WHITE PEPPER

PINCH OF NUTMEG

1 EGG YOLK

2 WHOLE BONELESS CHICKEN BREASTS,
  WITH FULL SKIN ON (ABOUT
  1½ POUNDS TOTAL)

2 TEASPOONS OLIVE OIL

**1.** In a small bowl, soak the raisins in the Madeira.

**2.** Combine the rice, 1 tablespoon of the butter, and 1 cup of water in a medium saucepan. Bring to a boil over high heat. Reduce the heat to low, cover, and cook for 20 minutes, or until all of the water is absorbed.

**3.** In a medium skillet, warm 3 tablespoons of the butter over medium heat until melted. Add the pecans and toss until lightly browned. Add the shallots and sauté until barely soft but not brown. Add the raisins with the Madeira and the orange peel and stir to mix well. Remove from the heat and add to the rice. Stir well. Add the salt, pepper, and nutmeg and stir to combine. Let the rice cool completely, then stir in the egg yolk.

**4.** Gently separate the chicken skin from the flesh. Fill the pockets with the rice stuffing. Smooth the skin over the rice so it is completely covered.

**5.** In a medium skillet, warm the oil with the remaining 2 teaspoons of butter over medium heat until the butter is melted. Add the chicken breasts, stuffed-side up, and sear over high heat for 2 minutes. Turn and sear 2 more minutes. If necessary, use tongs to hold the chicken and sear any raw edges. Reduce the heat to medium and sauté the breasts, stuffed-side up, for 10 to 12 minutes. Turn and cook for 5 minutes, or until the chicken is cooked through.

**6.** Transfer the chicken to a platter. Cut each breast in half and serve.

# STUFFED ROAST TURKEY

SERVES 6 TO 8

2 STICKS BUTTER

1 CUP CHOPPED SCALLIONS

1 CUP DICED CARROTS

3 GARLIC CLOVES, MINCED

1 POUND MUSHROOMS, FINELY
  CHOPPED

10 SLICES DAY-OLD WHOLE-WHEAT
  BREAD, CUT INTO CUBES

¼ CUP CHOPPED PARSLEY

1 TEASPOON THYME

3 TEASPOONS SALT

1½ TEASPOONS PEPPER

ONE 12-POUND TURKEY

1. Preheat the oven to 425°.

2. In a large skillet, warm 2 tablespoons of the butter over medium heat until melted. Add the scallions, carrots, and garlic, and sauté until the scallions are softened but not browned, about 5 minutes. Increase the heat to medium-high, add 6 tablespoons butter and the mushrooms, and sauté until the mushrooms are softened, 5 to 10 minutes.

3. Meanwhile, in a large bowl, combine the bread cubes, parsley, thyme, 1 teaspoon of salt, and ½ teaspoon pepper. Stir in the sautéed vegetables. Cool the stuffing slightly.

4. Stuff the turkey loosely and truss. Blend the remaining butter, salt, and pepper, and rub the outside of the turkey with the seasoned butter. Place the turkey, breast-side up, in a roasting pan and roast until golden brown, 30 to 35 minutes.

5. Turn the turkey on its side and baste with the pan juices. Lower the oven temperature to 350° and roast for 45 minutes, basting after about 20 minutes.

6. Turn the turkey onto its other side and baste with the pan juices. Roast for another 45 minutes, basting after about 20 minutes. Should any portion of the turkey seem to be browning too quickly, cover it loosely with foil.

7. The turkey is done when a meat thermometer inserted into the thickest part of the leg registers 180°. If the turkey is not done, roast it, breast-side up, for another 20 minutes, continuing to baste, and check again. Transfer the turkey to a carving board and let rest at least 15 minutes before carving.

# TURKEY BREAST PINWHEELS

### SERVES 10
### ♡ LOW-FAT

½ CUP MINCED PARSLEY

2 GARLIC CLOVES, MINCED

1 MEDIUM CARROT, COARSELY
 CHOPPED

1 CELERY RIB, COARSELY CHOPPED

¼ POUND MUSHROOMS, COARSELY
 CHOPPED

HALF A MEDIUM GRANNY SMITH
 APPLE, COARSELY CHOPPED

3 SCALLIONS, COARSELY CHOPPED

½ CUP COARSE FRESH BREAD CRUMBS

½ TEASPOON THYME

¼ TEASPOON BLACK PEPPER

2 TABLESPOONS CHICKEN BROTH

3 TABLESPOONS OLIVE OIL

1 TABLESPOON BUTTER

ONE 3¾-POUND SKINLESS, BONELESS
 TURKEY BREAST

½ TEASPOON SALT

**1.** Preheat the oven to 425°.

**2.** In a medium bowl, combine the parsley, garlic, carrot, celery, mushrooms, apple, scallions, bread crumbs, thyme, ⅛ teaspoon of the pepper, and the broth.

**3.** In a large skillet, warm 1 tablespoon of the oil with the butter over medium-high heat until the butter is melted. Add the contents of the bowl, and stir-fry for 5 minutes.

**4.** Put the turkey, skin-side down, on a work surface. With a sharp knife, cut a flap in the breast by slicing from the long, thin side toward the thicker side, being careful not to cut all the way through. Open the flap and place the turkey between two pieces of plastic wrap. With a mallet or rolling pin, pound lightly to an even thickness of about ½ inch.

**5.** Spread the stuffing mixture over the turkey breast. Starting at one long side, roll it up jelly-roll fashion. Place the rolled turkey, seam-side down, in the roasting pan.

**6.** In a small bowl, combine the remaining oil, parsley, and pepper, and the salt. Brush this over the turkey and roast it for 15 minutes. Reduce oven temperature to 300° and roast for 1¼ hours more, or until juices run clear. Baste the turkey several times with pan juices. Let the turkey rest for 10 minutes before carving into ¾-inch pinwheel slices.

# Wine-Roasted Cornish Game Hens

### SERVES 4

2 CORNISH GAME HENS (ABOUT 2
  POUNDS TOTAL), HALVED
¼ CUP DRY RED WINE
3 TABLESPOONS OLIVE OIL
2 GARLIC CLOVES, MINCED

2 TEASPOONS DIJON MUSTARD
½ TEASPOON ROSEMARY
½ TEASPOON SAGE
½ TEASPOON THYME
¼ TEASPOON BLACK PEPPER

**1.** Preheat the oven to 425°.

**2.** If the butcher has not split the hens for you, place them, breast-side up, on a work surface. With a sharp knife, cut all the way through the breasts, following the bone. Turn the hens over and cut through the backbones to halve them.

**3.** Place the halved hens in a single layer, skin-side up, in a baking dish or roasting pan.

**4.** In a small bowl, stir together the wine, oil, garlic, mustard, rosemary, sage, thyme, and pepper.

**5.** Pour the wine mixture over the hens. Place the hens in the oven and roast for 15 minutes.

**6.** Lower the oven temperature to 350° and roast until the juices run clear when the hens are pierced with the tip of a knife, about 45 minutes. Baste the hens every 15 minutes with the wine mixture.

**7.** Serve hen halves on individual dinner plates; spoon some of the pan juices on top.

**KITCHEN NOTE:** *Forget those supermarket "cooking wines," which are of poor quality and may have salt added to them. Always cook with a good, drinkable wine. For this recipe, you'll want to use a full-bodied red wine; you can serve the same wine with the meal.*

# ROAST DUCK STUFFED WITH PEARS AND GARLIC

SERVES 4

1 POUND SECKEL OR BOSC PEARS, CUT
   INTO ¾-INCH CUBES

1 TABLESPOON FRESH LIME JUICE

ONE 5-POUND DUCK

1 TABLESPOON BUTTER

15 TO 30 GARLIC CLOVES, PEELED

1 TABLESPOON CHOPPED FRESH
   ROSEMARY, OR 1 TEASPOON DRIED

1 TEASPOON SUGAR

1 TEASPOON SALT

1 BUNCH OF WATERCRESS, FOR
   GARNISH

**1.** In a medium bowl, toss the pears with the lime juice.

**2.** Trim any excess fat from around the neck of the duck. Remove any fat from the cavity. Cover the bottom of a large pot with 1 inch of water and set a metal rack in the pot. Bring the water to a boil over medium heat. Lightly prick the duck all over with a wooden pick or a skewer. Place the duck, breast-side down, in the pot. Reduce the heat to medium-low, cover, and steam the duck for 30 minutes.

**3.** Preheat the oven to 350°.

**4.** Warm the butter in a large skillet over medium heat until melted. Cook the garlic cloves in the butter, stirring frequently, until they begin to soften and brown, about 12 minutes. Stir in the pears, rosemary, and sugar, and cook until the pears are soft, about 8 minutes. Set aside.

**5.** When the duck has finished steaming, sprinkle it on the inside and outside with the salt. Place the duck on a rack in a roasting pan, breast-side down, and roast it for 15 minutes. Turn the duck, breast-side up, on the rack. Reduce the oven temperature to 325°. Prick the breast and legs of the duck. Fill the cavity with the pear-garlic mixture. Return the duck to the oven and roast until the skin turns a deep golden brown, about 1½ hours. Cut the duck into quarters and garnish with the watercress.

# ROAST DUCK WITH CRANBERRY-SAUSAGE STUFFING

SERVES 4 TO 6

3 TABLESPOONS BUTTER

½ POUND PORK SAUSAGE, CASINGS REMOVED

2 GARLIC CLOVES, MINCED

1 CUP CHOPPED SCALLIONS

1 CUP CHOPPED CELERY

1¾ CUPS FRESH CRANBERRIES—¾ CUP CHOPPED AND 1 CUP WHOLE

1 CUP APRICOT PRESERVES

2 TABLESPOONS CHOPPED PARSLEY

¾ TEASPOON THYME

½ TEASPOON SALT

¼ TEASPOON BLACK PEPPER

3 CUPS COOKED RICE

ONE 5-POUND DUCK, RINSED

2 TABLESPOONS FRESH LEMON JUICE

1 TEASPOON SALT

¼ CUP CHOPPED SHALLOTS OR ONION

**1.** Preheat the oven to 475°.

**2.** In a large skillet, warm 2 tablespoons of the butter over medium heat until melted. Add the sausage and half of the garlic and sauté, breaking up the meat with a spoon, for 5 minutes. Add the scallions, celery, chopped cranberries, ½ cup of apricot preserves, the parsley, thyme, salt, and pepper, and cook, stirring, for 10 minutes. Stir in the rice.

**3.** Fill the cavity of the duck loosely with about half of the stuffing. Place the remaining stuffing in a greased baking dish, cover, and set aside. Truss the duck, rub with the lemon juice, and sprinkle with the salt. Prick the duck all over with a fork and place it, breast-side up, on a rack in a roasting pan.

**4.** Roast the duck for 15 minutes. Lower the temperature to 350° and continue roasting until the duck is golden brown and a meat thermometer inserted into the thickest part of the leg registers 180°, about 1½ hours. About 30 minutes before the duck is done, place the baking dish of stuffing in the oven and bake.

**5.** In a small saucepan, warm the remaining butter over medium heat until melted. Add the shallots and remaining garlic and sauté for 5 minutes. Add the whole cranberries and the remaining apricot preserves and cook, stirring, for 5 minutes. Let the mixture cool slightly and then purée in a food processor.

**6.** Serve the duck with the stuffing and the sauce on the side.

# BEEF TENDERLOIN ROAST WITH SPINACH SAUCE

SERVES 6

4 TEASPOONS SAFFLOWER OIL
1¾ POUNDS BEEF TENDERLOIN ROAST
¼ TEASPOON SALT
2 PINCHES OF BLACK PEPPER
2 TABLESPOONS SLIVERED ALMONDS
3 TABLESPOONS FINELY CHOPPED
    SHALLOTS

1 CUP DRY WHITE WINE
½ POUND SPINACH
¼ CUP SKIM MILK
⅛ TEASPOON NUTMEG

1. Preheat the oven to 325°.

2. In a large nonstick skillet, heat 1 teaspoon of the oil over high heat. Sear the meat in the skillet until it is browned on all sides, 2 to 3 minutes. Season the meat with ⅛ teaspoon of the salt and a pinch of pepper. Transfer the tenderloin to a roasting pan; do not wash the skillet. Finish cooking the meat in the oven, about 35 minutes, or until a meat thermometer inserted in the center registers 140°.

3. In a small nonstick skillet, toast the almonds over medium heat, stirring constantly, until they are lightly browned, about 2 to 3 minutes.

4. Heat the remaining tablespoon of oil in the large skillet over medium heat. Add the shallots and cook them until they are translucent, about 2 minutes. Pour in the wine and simmer the liquid until about ⅓ cup remains, 6 to 8 minutes. Add the spinach and reduce the heat to low. Cover the pan and cook the spinach until it has wilted, 1 to 2 minutes. Stir in the milk and nutmeg. Return the mixture to a simmer, then transfer it to a food processor or blender and purée it. Season the sauce with the remaining salt and a pinch of pepper.

5. Let the tenderloin rest 10 minutes before carving into 12 slices. Arrange the slices on a warmed serving platter, spoon some of the sauce over them, and sprinkle with the almonds. Pass the remaining sauce separately.

# LONDON BROIL WITH RED WINE MARINADE

### SERVES 4

½ CUP DRY RED WINE, PREFERABLY
    BURGUNDY
1 LARGE GARLIC CLOVE, CRUSHED
¼ CUP VEGETABLE OIL
¼ TEASPOON BLACK PEPPER

½ TEASPOON DIJON MUSTARD
⅛ TEASPOON THYME
1¾ POUNDS LONDON BROIL
1 SMALL BUNCH OF WATERCRESS

**1.** In a medium bowl, combine the wine, garlic, oil, pepper, mustard, and thyme.

**2.** With a fork, pierce the meat deeply about a dozen times on each side. Place the meat in a glass baking dish just large enough to hold it. Pour the marinade over the meat and turn once to coat. Cover the dish and refrigerate for at least 1 hour, or overnight, turning the meat once or twice.

**3.** Preheat the broiler.

**4.** Remove the meat from the marinade and place on a broiler pan. Broil the meat for 5 minutes on each side for medium-rare, or until desired doneness.

**5.** Transfer the meat to a warmed platter and allow to rest for 10 minutes. Cut the meat across the grain into slices about ¼ inch thick. Garnish with sprigs of watercress.

**Variation:** *You can grill the steak instead of broiling it. Be extra-careful, though, not to leave the steak over the coals for too long—London broil (flank steak) can be tough if it's overcooked.*

# FILET MIGNON WITH POTATOES AND LEEKS

SERVES 4

♡ LOW-FAT

⅛ TEASPOON SALT

½ TEASPOON ROSEMARY

½ TEASPOON THYME

¼ TEASPOON BLACK PEPPER

3 GARLIC CLOVES—1 MINCED AND 2 PEELED

4 FILET MIGNON STEAKS (½ INCH THICK, ABOUT 14 OUNCES TOTAL)

1½ POUNDS SMALL RED POTATOES

2½ TEASPOONS OLIVE OIL

4 LEEKS, HALVED LENGTHWISE AND CUT INTO 2-INCH PIECES

2 RED BELL PEPPERS, CUT INTO 1-INCH SQUARES

1. In a small bowl, combine ¼ teaspoon of the salt, the rosemary, thyme, pepper, and minced garlic. Rub the mixture into the steaks; set aside.

2. Preheat the oven to 425°. With a vegetable peeler, remove a thin band of skin around the center of each potato. In a large pot of boiling water, cook the potatoes for 10 minutes (potatoes will not be tender). Drain and pat dry.

3. In a large baking pan, combine the oil and peeled garlic and heat in the oven. Add the potatoes, tossing to coat. Roast for 10 minutes, or until lightly golden. Add the leeks and bell peppers, tossing to coat. Sprinkle with the remaining ½ teaspoon salt and roast for another 10 minutes, or until the vegetables are almost tender.

4. Meanwhile, spray a large skillet with nonstick cooking spray, then heat over medium-high heat. Add the steaks and cook until lightly browned on the bottoms, about 2 minutes. Place the steaks, browned-side up, on top of the vegetables and continue to roast for 7 minutes for medium-rare steaks, or until desired doneness. Divide the steaks and vegetables among 4 plates and serve.

# ROAST BEEF WITH CLOVES AND RED PEPPERS

SERVES 12

2 RED BELL PEPPERS
3½ POUNDS SIRLOIN TIP ROAST
1 TEASPOON GROUND CLOVES
1 TABLESPOON SAFFLOWER OIL
½ TEASPOON SALT

⅛ TEASPOON BLACK PEPPER
1 CUP BEEF BROTH, PREFERABLY
   REDUCED-SODIUM
2 MEDIUM ONIONS
½ CUP DRY WHITE WINE

**1.** Preheat the broiler. Roast the bell peppers on a baking sheet in the broiler, turning them as their skins blister, until they are blackened on all sides, about 15 minutes. Transfer the peppers to a bowl and cover to allow the steam to loosen the skins.

**2.** Sprinkle the roast all over with ½ teaspoon of the cloves.

**3.** In a large nonstick skillet, warm the oil over high heat. Add the beef and sear it until it is well browned on all sides, about 5 minutes. Transfer the beef to a shallow baking dish and sprinkle it with ¼ teaspoon of the salt and the black pepper.

**4.** Roast the beef for 1 hour. If the meat juices begin to blacken in the bottom of the baking dish, pour in a few tablespoons of the broth.

**5.** While the roast is cooking, peel the peppers, working over a bowl to catch the juice. Strain the juice and set it aside. Slice the peppers into strips about 1 inch long and ½ inch wide. Cut the onions in half from top to bottom, then slice them with the grain into strips roughly the same size as the pepper strips.

**6.** When the roast has cooked for 1 hour, add to the baking dish the peppers and their juice, the onions, broth, wine, remaining ½ teaspoon of cloves, and the remaining ¼ teaspoon of salt. Cook the beef for 30 minutes, or until a meat thermometer inserted in the center of the roast registers 140°.

**7.** Cut the meat into thin slices and arrange them on a platter, surrounded by the vegetables. Drizzle any sauce remaining in the baking dish over the meat and serve.

# FRENCH-STYLE ROAST BEEF

SERVES 6

♡ LOW-FAT

1 CUP WHITE GRAPE JUICE

½ CUP DRY WHITE WINE

2 TABLESPOONS BRANDY

1 TABLESPOON WHITE WINE VINEGAR

1 LARGE ONION, SLICED

3 MEDIUM CARROTS, SLICED

1 LARGE GARLIC CLOVE, CHOPPED

1 BAY LEAF

1 SPRIG OF ROSEMARY

3 OR 4 SPRIGS OF THYME

2 LARGE SPRIGS OF PARSLEY

6 BLACK PEPPERCORNS, CRUSHED

½ TEASPOON SALT

1½ POUNDS BEEF TOP ROUND, CUT INTO 1-INCH CUBES

3 TABLESPOONS OLIVE OIL

TWO 14-OUNCE CANS CHOPPED TOMATOES

½ POUND MUSHROOMS, SLICED

1 STRIP ORANGE ZEST

2 OUNCES PROSCIUTTO, CUT INTO STRIPS

12 BLACK OLIVES

**1.** In a large bowl, combine the grape juice, wine, brandy, vinegar, onion, carrots, garlic, bay leaf, rosemary, thyme, parsley, peppercorns, and salt. Add the beef and toss to combine. Cover the bowl and refrigerate for 8 to 12 hours, stirring 2 or 3 times.

**2.** Preheat the oven to 300°. Drain the meat, reserving the marinade, and pat the cubes dry with paper towels. In a large nonstick skillet warm 1 tablespoon of the oil over high heat. Add about ⅓ of the meat and cook until the pieces are well browned on all sides, 2 to 3 minutes. Transfer the meat to a large casserole. Brown the remaining beef in 2 batches in the same way, adding more oil, if necessary.

**3.** Pour the reserved marinade over the meat, add the chopped tomatoes, and stir. Bring the mixture to a boil, cover the casserole tightly, and bake for 2½ hours.

**4.** Add the mushrooms, orange zest, prosciutto, and olives, and cook for 30 minutes more, or until the beef is very tender. If there is a lot of excess liquid at this stage, cook uncovered.

**5.** Transfer the beef to a platter and spoon the vegetables and pan juices over the top.

# GERMAN-STYLE ROAST PORK

SERVES 4

2 TABLESPOONS MINCED GARLIC

1 TABLESPOON GRATED LEMON ZEST

1 SMALL BUNCH FRESH MARJORAM,
  COARSELY CHOPPED, OR
  ½ TEASPOON DRIED

½ TEASPOON SALT

1 TABLESPOON CARAWAY SEEDS

¼ TEASPOON BLACK PEPPER

1¾ POUNDS BONELESS CENTER LOIN
  PORK ROAST, CUT IN HALF

½ CUP DICED CARROT

¼ CUP DICED ONION

½ CUP DICED CELERY

1 CUP DARK BEER

¾ CUP CHICKEN BROTH

1 BAY LEAF

1 TABLESPOON CORNSTARCH BLENDED
  WITH 2 TABLESPOONS WATER

**1.** Preheat the oven to 475°.

**2.** In a small bowl or mortar, combine the garlic, lemon zest, marjoram, salt, caraway seeds, and pepper, and grind finely with the back of a wooden spoon or pestle. Rub the spice mixture into the tenderloin.

**3.** Scatter the carrot, onion, and celery over the bottom of a lightly oiled roasting pan. Top with the pork and drizzle with 2 tablespoons of the dark beer. Place the pork in the oven and roast for 20 minutes. Reduce the oven temperature to 400°. If most of the liquid has evaporated, add ¼ cup of chicken broth. Continue roasting the pork another 30 minutes. The pork is done when the juices run clear when pierced with a skewer or when a meat thermometer registers 170°. Transfer the pork to a platter and cover with foil.

**4.** Place the roasting pan on the stove over medium-high heat. Add the remaining beer and the bay leaf and scrape up any brown bits clinging to the bottom of the plan. Cook until the liquid is reduced by about half, 5 to 7 minutes. Increase the heat to high, add the remaining broth, and bring the mixture to a boil. Reduce the heat to medium and simmer for 5 minutes.

**5.** Stirring constantly, gradually add the cornstarch mixture to the pan. Pour the sauce through a coarse strainer set over a small bowl, pressing with the back of a spoon to squeeze out as much liquid as possible. Discard the solids left in the strainer.

**6.** Cut each pork loin into thin slices and serve on a platter, drizzled with the sauce.

# POT-ROASTED PORK LOIN WITH CHERRY TOMATOES

SERVES 6

1 TABLESPOON OLIVE OIL

1½ POUNDS PORK LOIN, BONED

2 TEASPOONS FENNEL SEEDS

1 TEASPOON BLACK PEPPERCORNS

2 TABLESPOONS WHITE WINE VINEGAR

2 TABLESPOONS WHITE WINE

¼ TEASPOON SALT

½ POUND CHERRY TOMATOES, PEELED

**1.** In a heatproof casserole that is just large enough to hold the pork loin, warm the oil over medium heat. Add the pork and lightly brown the meat all over, about 6 minutes.

**2.** Pour off and discard the oil, then add the fennel seeds, peppercorns, vinegar, wine, and salt to the casserole. Cover and cook over low heat for 1 hour; check the level of the liquid occasionally and add more vinegar and wine if necessary. About 10 minutes before the end of cooking, add the tomatoes to the casserole.

**3.** Carefully remove the meat from the casserole and cut into ¼-inch-thick slices. Overlap the slices in the middle of a warmed serving dish and arrange the tomatoes along the edges of the dish. Skim the fat from the surface of the liquid in the casserole, then pour the juices over the meat, making sure to include the fennel seeds and peppercorns.

**KITCHEN NOTE:** *Don't panic at the thought of peeling a half-pound of cherry tomatoes—it's easier than you might think. Bring a large pot of water to a boil. Drop in the tomatoes and blanch them just until their skins start to wrinkle and split (about 20 seconds). Drain the tomatoes and spread them on a plate to cool slightly, then remove the skins—they'll slip right off.*

# VEAL STROGANOFF

SERVES 4

¼ CUP DRIED MUSHROOMS

1 POUND EGG NOODLES

¼ CUP PAPRIKA

1 TEASPOON SALT

2 TEASPOONS BLACK PEPPER

2 POUNDS VEAL (FROM LEG ROUND ROAST), CUT INTO STRIPS

1 STICK PLUS 4 TABLESPOONS BUTTER

2 GARLIC CLOVES, MINCED

1 MEDIUM ONION, FINELY CHOPPED

ONE 6-OUNCE CAN TOMATO PASTE

½ CUP VODKA

2 TABLESPOONS POPPY SEEDS

¼ CUP CHOPPED PARSLEY

1 TABLESPOON FRESH LEMON JUICE

1 CUP SOUR CREAM

1. Place the mushrooms in a medium bowl and cover with 2 cups of boiling water. Soak for 15 to 20 minutes. Drain the mushrooms in a sieve set over a medium bowl, reserving the soaking liquid. Finely chop the mushrooms.

2. Bring a large pot of water to a boil. Cook the noodles for about 9 minutes, or according to the package directions.

3. Meanwhile, on wax paper, mix the paprika, salt, and pepper. Dredge the veal strips in the mixture.

4. In a Dutch oven, warm 1 stick of the butter over medium heat until it turns amber. Add the veal in small batches and brown evenly. Transfer the veal to a heatproof platter and keep warm in the oven.

5. To the Dutch oven add the garlic, onion, and mushrooms and cook over medium heat for 5 minutes, stirring occasionally. Add the tomato paste and vodka and bring to a boil, stirring frequently. Add the veal, reduce the heat to medium, and cook for 10 to 15 minutes, stirring occasionally.

6. In a small saucepan, heat the remaining 4 tablespoons of butter. In a medium bowl, toss the butter with the cooked noodles, the poppy seeds, and parsley.

7. In a small bowl, mix the lemon juice with the sour cream. Remove the Dutch oven from the heat and stir in the sour cream mixture.

8. Transfer the noodles to a large platter, top with the veal mixture, and serve.

# ROAST LEG OF LAMB WITH ROSEMARY BUTTER

SERVES 4

ONE 5-POUND LEG OF LAMB, TRIMMED
    AND BUTTERFLIED
2 TABLESPOONS VEGETABLE OIL
2 TABLESPOONS CHOPPED FRESH
    ROSEMARY

½ TEASPOON SALT
¼ TEASPOON PEPPER
1 STICK UNSALTED BUTTER
3 TABLESPOONS DIJON MUSTARD

**1.** Preheat the broiler.

**2.** Rub the lamb all over with the oil and 1 tablespoon of the rosemary. Sprinkle with the salt and pepper.

**3.** Place the lamb, skin-side up, on a broiler pan and broil 6 inches from the heat for 20 minutes. Using a long, double-pronged fork, turn the lamb and broil another 15 minutes.

**4.** Meanwhile, in a small saucepan, melt the butter with the remaining rosemary. Add the mustard and remove from the heat. Whisk until the mustard is incorporated and the mixture binds together.

**5.** When the lamb is done, transfer it to a carving board and let it rest a few minutes. Cut the lamb into thin slices. Spoon the sauce over the slices just before serving.

KITCHEN NOTE: *A butterflied leg is a thick cut of lamb that has been boned and then carefully cut so that it can be opened out into a large, flat piece. Once shaped, the meat is pounded to an even thickness. Although it's possible to butterfly a leg of lamb yourself, you're better off leaving this job to the butcher.*

# Roast Salmon with Mushroom-Rice Stuffing

SERVES 4

♡ LOW - FAT

1 TEASPOON OLIVE OIL

3 SCALLIONS, THINLY SLICED

1 GARLIC CLOVE, MINCED

2 CUPS SLICED BUTTON MUSHROOMS

2 CUPS SLICED SHIITAKE MUSHROOMS

⅔ CUP LONG-GRAIN WHITE RICE

¾ TEASPOON SALT

¾ TEASPOON TARRAGON

¾ TEASPOON ROSEMARY

1¾ POUNDS CENTER-CUT SALMON
   FILLET

¼ CUP FRESH LEMON JUICE

1 TEASPOON CORNSTARCH, BLENDED
   WITH 1 CUP WATER

¼ CUP MINCED FRESH DILL

½ TEASPOON DIJON MUSTARD

**1.** In a large saucepan, warm the oil over medium heat. Add the scallions and garlic and cook, stirring frequently, until softened, about 2 minutes. Stir in all the mushrooms. Add ¼ cup of water and cook, stirring frequently, until the mushrooms are tender, about 7 minutes. Stir in the rice, 1½ cups of water, ½ teaspoon of the salt, ½ teaspoon of the tarragon, and ½ teaspoon of the rosemary and bring to a boil. Reduce the heat to medium-low, cover, and simmer until the rice is tender, about 20 minutes. Transfer to a small roasting pan, fluff with a fork, and cool for 10 minutes.

**2.** Preheat the oven to 425°. Lay the salmon flat, flesh-side up, and rub with the remaining ¼ teaspoon each salt, tarragon, and rosemary. Place the salmon, skin-side up, over the stuffing. With a small paring knife, lightly score the skin and roast for 20 to 25 minutes, or until the salmon is just opaque.

**3.** Meanwhile, in a small saucepan, bring the lemon juice and 2 tablespoons of water to a boil over medium heat. Add the cornstarch-water mixture and cook, stirring constantly, until the sauce is slightly thickened, about 1 minute. Remove from the heat and stir in the dill and mustard. Divide the salmon among 4 serving plates, spoon the sauce on top, and serve with the stuffing.

# STUFFED LOBSTER

SERVES 4

♡ LOW-FAT

6 SLICES DAY-OLD BREAD, CRUMBLED
  INTO SMALL PIECES
2 TABLESPOONS OLIVE OIL
2 SHALLOTS, FINELY CHOPPED, OR
  ¼ CUP FINELY CHOPPED ONION
¼ CUP CHOPPED FRESH OREGANO,
  MARJORAM, OR ITALIAN PARSLEY

6 GARLIC CLOVES, FINELY CHOPPED
⅛ TEASPOON BLACK PEPPER
⅓ CUP FRESH LEMON JUICE
2 TEASPOONS PAPRIKA, PREFERABLY
  HUNGARIAN
4 LIVE LOBSTERS (ABOUT 5 POUNDS
  TOTAL)

**1.** In a large bowl, combine the bread, oil, shallots, half of the oregano, half of the garlic, and the pepper. Set aside.

**2.** In a small bowl, combine the remaining oregano and garlic with the lemon juice and paprika.

**3.** Preheat the oven to 500°.

**4.** Kill the lobsters by plunging them into a large pot of boiling water for 1 minute. Remove the lobsters with tongs and let them drain until they are cool enough to handle. Twist off the claws. Using a large, heavy knife, split each lobster down the entire length of the body and tail. Remove the greenish tomalley with a spoon and chop it. Add the tomalley to the stuffing and mix well. Remove the viscera from the stomach cavity and discard them along with the thin side claws.

**5.** Arrange the lobster halves in a large baking dish with their cut sides up. Gently crack the claws and arrange them around the tails. Loosely fill the stomach cavities with the stuffing. Drizzle the lemon juice mixture over the tail meat only and place the baking dish in the oven. Bake the lobsters until the stuffing is lightly browned on top, about 12 to 15 minutes.

**6.** Transfer the lobsters (not the claws) to a large serving platter and cover them with foil to keep warm. Return the claws to the oven and bake for 5 minutes. Arrange the claws around the lobsters and serve.

# MENU SUGGESTIONS

# Welcome, Neighbors!

Spinach Salad with Mushrooms
and Croutons (page 60)

Pennsylvania Dutch Chicken
(page 9)

Baked Corn
(page 42)

Butter-Walnut Baked Pears and Apples
(page 84)

# The Boss Comes to Dinner

Tossed Green Salad with
Sherry Vinegar Dressing (page 58)

Veal Stroganoff
(page 113)

Green Beans in Shallot Butter
(page 46)

Almond-Fruit Tart
(page 85)

# Old Friends in Town

### Greek Salad
(PAGE 69)

### Roast Leg of Lamb
### with Rosemary Butter (PAGE 114)

### Sautéed Apple Slices
(PAGE 55)

### Orange Carrot Cake
(PAGE 94)

# A Touch of Mardi Gras

### Green Salad with
### Lemon-Mustard Vinaigrette (PAGE 61)

### French-Style Roast Beef (PAGE 110)

### Scalloped New Potatoes
(PAGE 34)

### New Orleans Bread Pudding
### with Bourbon Sauce (PAGE 91)

# THE KIDS COOK DINNER

MARINATED TOMATO
AND RED ONION SALAD
(PAGE 63)

CHICKEN POT PIE
(PAGE 11)

APPLE CAKE
(PAGE 96)

# SPRING CELEBRATION

CAESAR SALAD (PAGE 57)

ROAST SALMON WITH
MUSHROOM-RICE STUFFING (PAGE 115)

CAULIFLOWER-CHEDDAR GRATIN
(PAGE 38)

STRAWBERRY CHEESECAKE PIE
(PAGE 79)

# Happy Anniversary!

Marinated Mushroom Salad
(PAGE 73)

Roast Pork Loin with Sage
(PAGE 16)

Glazed Carrot Coins
(PAGE 37)

Tennessee Black Cake
(PAGE 81)

# Family Reunion

German-Style Roast Pork
(PAGE 111)

Pennsylvania German-Style Broccoli
(PAGE 35)

Stuffed Baked Potatoes
(PAGE 48)

Apple Crumb Pie
(PAGE 76)

# Backyard Picnic

Marinated Zucchini Salad
(PAGE 59)

Southern Fried Chicken
(PAGE 10)

Spoon Bread
(PAGE 53)

Open-Faced Peach Pie
(PAGE 89)

# At the Beach House

Avocado Salad
(PAGE 62)

Stuffed Lobster
(PAGE 116)

Fried Green Tomatoes
(PAGE 41)

Peanut Butter Cup Pie
(PAGE 82)

# Back-to-School Special

Cucumber Salad with Sour Cream
(PAGE 68)

Cider-Glazed Fresh Ham
(PAGE 20)

Cheddar Drop Biscuits
(PAGE 52)

Rice Pudding with Dried Fruit
(PAGE 87)

# Autumn Homecoming

Green Bean, Red Onion, and Bacon Salad
(PAGE 66)

Turkey Breast Pinwheels
(PAGE 102)

Creamed Yams with Brown Sugar
(PAGE 49)

Cranberry-Apple Pandowdy
(PAGE 80)

# HUNGRY HIKERS' TREAT

RED AND GREEN CABBAGE SALAD
(PAGE 67)

COUNTRY MEAT LOAF
(PAGE 24)

PARMESAN POTATOES
(PAGE 36)

BLUEBERRY CRUMBLE
(PAGE 83)

# LET'S CELEBRATE!

CARROT, APPLE, AND WALNUT SALAD
(PAGE 71)

ROAST CHICKEN WITH STUFFING
(PAGE 8)

CREAMED SPINACH
(PAGE 43)

BLUEBERRY-CHERRY COBBLER
(PAGE 90)

# FOR GOOD REPORT CARDS

Tossed Salad with Parmesan Dressing
(PAGE 65)

Pork Chops with
Yam and Sausage Stuffing (PAGE 18)

Tart Applesauce
(PAGE 56)

One-Pan Chocolate Walnut Cake
(PAGE 92)

# SNOWED IN

Yankee Pot Roast
(PAGE 23)

Garlic Mashed Potatoes
(PAGE 32)

Wax Beans and Cherry Tomatoes
(PAGE 40)

Chocolate Chip-Almond Pound Cake
(PAGE 78)

# Index